SYSTEMATIC NETWORKING

SYSTEMATIC NETWORKING:
A Guide for
Personal and Corporate
Success

Roger Hayes

CASSELL

Cassell
Wellington House, 125 Strand, London WC2R 0BB
127 West 24th Street, New York, NY 10011

© Roger Hayes 1996

First published 1996

British Library Cataloguing-in-Publication Data
A catalogue record for this book is available from the British Library.

ISBN 0-304-33813-3 (hardback)
0-304-33814-1 (paperback)

Designed and typeset by Kenneth Burnley at Irby, Wirral, Cheshire.
Printed and bound in Great Britain by Redwood Books, Trowbridge, Wiltshire.

Contents

Acknowledgements

I am indebted to Nicky Hirsch who undertook some of the interviews and research as well as a constant stream of ideas; to Tamsin Edwards from Australia and Molly Pagett in America who provided information and intelligence; to Penelope Denson who assisted with the text; and to Mike Johnson for drawing the cartoons.

Dedicated to

Nicolas

who will need to more than ever,
but will be better prepared than I was.

Definitions

'To interact with others for mutual assistance or support.'
The American Heritage Dictionary of the English Language

'Two or more intelligent devices linked in order to exchange
information and share resources.'   Digital Equipment Corporation

'Networking is like a spider's web. When something lands
in it vibrations are sent out along it . . . a whole range
of processes result from people being interlinked with each other.'
David Clutterbuck, Management writer and trainer

Introduction

'Chance favours the prepared mind.'   Louis Pasteur

I would never have thought of writing a book on this subject unless the publishers had asked me, even though I have always considered myself quite good at it, whatever *it* is; and others, whom I respect, have always considered me, whatever my faults, to be a good networker. One former boss once said of me that he did not know how I pulled it off, but somehow I did. On reflection a key element of 'pulling it off' was largely to do with networking, although neither he nor I would every have described it as such. Another friend and former colleague once said that, if nothing else, he would always use me to get through to the right person, even if I did not know them. And that is the point: usually you don't and I certainly didn't in those days, hence the importance of networking.

Another friend and former supplier always argues that my most important professional talent is the ability to put the best teams together to produce a result, which is a characteristic of networking. Another has said that in the creative, ideas world in which I reside, the ability to bring together two otherwise unconnected pieces of information to solve a puzzle is my Unique Selling Proposition (USP) (if I have one), another spin-off of networking. Even so I would never have produced a book on networking, as there are many other areas where I have a passionate interest and even experience. Yet the very week when the publishers popped the question, I had a visit from an author who had been recommended to ask me about networking. So perhaps there's something in it after all.

I started life as a journalist, I have been a public relations consultant, worked in management consulting, been involved in British politics, lived and worked in France and America as well as the UK, handled corporate, investor, political and media affairs for a variety of organizations all over the world, been active in many networks, built and sold a company; and I currently sit on a variety of boards and head up a trade association, the sole rationale for which is information and influence. I should therefore know something about the subject. I believe I do, but it wasn't until I started my own small company and began to build it that networking for me really came into its own in a conscious way. Some argue I have netweaved as much as networked, meaning linking individuals within networks and joining together networks to create new ones. The irony is that to network requires you to belong to one already. The problem is people probably don't realize they already do: they just haven't analyzed it and made it work for them. But it is true that while most people are passive, netweavers are proactive in making the connections and linkages that can keep them in their corporation or personal careers. By definition, networking cannot be undertaken in a vacuum. What having my own company did was force me to put it onto a systematic basis, integrate it with other aspects of the team's marketing and promotional activity and even build it into the campaigns and programmes of clients.

It requires energy and graft and discipline to get it right. I recall over the years from a variety of perspectives how badly companies and professionals sometimes do it. We all learn from our mistakes, but in networking at least, some organizations and individuals never seem to learn the lessons. Two examples will suffice. For years I was invited to lunches and other more elaborate functions in a stylish way to persuade me to buy an organization's products and services. While the events were usually brilliantly organized, the other guests were always other public relations, advertising and corporate affairs executives, whom I could just as easily meet in other settings. Not that the events themselves were not interesting or fun; they certainly were. But with a little more insight and thought into what networking really is, the sponsors would have realized that people in those positions want to meet people in other walks of life in the circle of opinion-forming. A public relations executive wants to meet a journalist or a securities analyst, a chief executive, a politician or official.

I recall another firm in Australia, with a London and New York office, which with just a little bit more effort and digging could have pulled together a brilliant mix of people, rather than just an average one, to celebrate an anniversary. They had all the ingredients under the marquee, but they just didn't make that extra effort and investment. Table planning ('Placements') is an art-form – knowing enough about your guests' interests and the pecking order to 'mix and match' correctly. Networking is about making the connections, forging the links in the spider's web, all of which requires a cross-flow of information, research and databasing ('hot linking' is the buzz term). How few companies have anything more than their Christmas card list to work from.

I remember too one company I was connected with which sent the same Christmas card to the same individuals from a variety of sources in the same office, with no cross-check. It always surprises me that once you leave a company's employ how soon you are dropped from the mailing list, even though you are likely to end up at a later date wearing a different hat. Of course you are soon back on the mailing list once you become a client!

The point here is not to bite the hand that feeds you, to be ungrateful for past jobs or invites, simply to illustrate how much more effective networking can be if it's undertaken *proactively, systematically* and *coherently* within a disciplined framework. This applies as much to companies, especially small businesses, as it does to individual professionals. This book will argue that even large businesses increasingly need to network, that individuals achieve more the younger they start, that women have to become adept at it (indeed are), and that the best time to build up 'social capital' (adding value through other people, which is what networking is all about), is before you need it, before you lose your job or set up in self-employment. Within companies, a networked manager is better able to get the right people together to take advantage of opportunities. People who just work within their 'cluster' are less likely to be as beneficial to a company as those who see the connections (however weak) to other clusters positioned at the crossroads between social clusters within the firm and its market. People better connected across structural holes (disconnections) are better positioned to broker otherwise difficult or unlikely exchanges and so enjoy higher returns on their human capital.

It fascinates me that so many professional people, often rich and successful, either as a result of the triumph of massive single-mindedness over broader vision, or usually confusing the urgent with what's important, fail to return phone calls. A key ingredient in the networking process (and that is what it is, a process, as the first chapter describes), is those individuals or organizations who beat a path to your door because they inevitably want something, usually a piece of information, which you can trade. It is all about mutuality and referral, an investment in the future. Even rich and successful people may suffer a turn of fortune; see how quickly their influence wanes if they have failed to nurture their network.

Colleagues in the UK and even America, where networking is taken more seriously and where I spend part of my time, have told me that networking is not susceptible to definition, codification, diagnosis or methodology because it simply *is*. It is a bit like sex appeal; you either have 'it' or you don't. It requires flair and you must have something worth sell-ing but it can be taught and there are approaches to it. Some believe it smacks of over-egging what is an intuitive, natural part of human relations. I certainly do not intend to take myself or this subject too seriously, but it is important nevertheless. I certainly believe it is about building relation-ships, but surely in a business, professional context, whether you are the CEO of a large corporation needing to co-operate as much as to compete (a competitor one minute is an alliance the next), whether you are a virtual company punching above your weight in partnership with others, a small business building up your contacts, an individual networking informally internally within an organization, or an independent individual (whether forcibly or by choice), networking must be a vital part of your armoury. Of course, it can be misconstrued if handled too brashly and counterproduc-tive if the wrong attitude prevails. This goes to the heart of the argument. My proposition is that networking is not superficial, cosmetic, transaction-based, a quick fix. On the contrary, I contend that for networking to work requires an investment of time and energy. Rather like President Kennedy's famous inauguration quote 'Ask not what your *country* can do for *you* . . .', it is important to make a contribution for a corporate or personal network to work. How many times do you hear people say, 'What's in it for me?' To achieve 'networth', whether in terms of financial or emotional equity, a commitment is required. Unlike the transaction-driven, short-term, indi-vidually-motivated mind-set of the 1980s, I genuinely believe that the 1990s and the new millennium will truly be the Age of the Network, where 'social capital' – the capacity for members of an economic group to forge trust and recognize their mutual interests – will gain importance as a spur to a greater sense of community and economic growth in the West.

Most of the literature reviews different network structures, mainly within corporations, and there are primers on how to work the room or win friends and influence people. Like all adventures I didn't know where this book would end up, but what it has tried to achieve is to draw the threads together of a whole variety of corporate and individual experiences from around the world, concentrating more on the goals, the strategy rather than the tactics. The book has covered some ground in the area of targeting and how to expand the sphere of influence, both of which are inter-related as is the information on which it is based. But even before dealing with interfaces and influence, a precursor is assessing what are the key issues of interest or necessity for life, job, company and the like.

This is not a 'How-to' book, although there are some pointers, ultimately. Rather it sets the networking phenomenon in the context of the fast-changing environment where knowledge, autonomous employment, new patterns of information flow, flatter structures and relationships provide more networking opportunities if at the same time greater complexity. A mix of case studies and mentoring are used to press home the points, that ultimately networking is about relationships not transactions, about trust rather than trade, about long term not short term, with people and communication at the centre.

1 Voyage Around the Web: Network Environment

'Your power is almost directly proportional to the thickness
of your Rolodex and the time you spend maintaining it . . .
The most potent people know everybody from everywhere
and have just been to lunch with most of them.'   Tom Peters

'If you like walking in quicksand, you'll love managing
in the twenty-first century.'   Tom Peters

It has always been the age of the networker; it's just that in an age of management gurus and marketing buzzwords it has taken on a life of its own. I
happen to believe, supported by research and experience, that networking
is less than a pure science – but an art at which gifted amateurs can easily
succeed, if they pursue it systematically.

Tom Peters with his usual enthusiasm exaggerates to make two points
which are true in part – knowing more people rather than fewer is obviously better as a general rule; and having lunch, so long as lunch is
managed, is part of the process. In my definition networking is more targeted than that. It is wide and deep depending on the appropriate tactic for
the strategic purpose in question. In any definition a *true* network is one
that works for the professional individual or organization while it is out to
supper or sleeping afterwards, simply because so much 'social capital' has
been expended on it. This book refers to networking for *networth*. But to
become *networthy* requires of the networker *trustworthiness*, a constant
theme throughout the text. Many 'networking notables' to whom I talked
referred to the mutual, reciprocal nature of the networking relationship,
based on trust. Indeed in mythology, whenever networking is referred to, it
is in the context of 'binding', the glue that binds.

If it has always been the age of the networker, intuitive and subcon-
scious, it is now more vital than ever to use it to mutual advantage, to make
it a way of life. After the greedy 1980s we are living in the decent 1990s
with individual and corporate value systems changing, where people and
communications are at the centre and in which networking naturally fits.

A famous British advertising guru, a member of the 'schmoozeoisie', used to send bouquets of flowers to government ministers after cabinet reshuffles, which sometimes annoyed competitors who believed that they did not have to wine and dine the good and the great so long as they were thinking about their clients' business. One approach may be a little eccentric and the retort necessary but insufficient. To be frank, different approaches are needed over a long period of time, the key to which is targeting over a sustained period. Sustainable success requires continuity as well as consistency and coherence.

Even within companies, in an era when organizations depend more and more on tenuously connected insiders and increasingly outsiders to get the

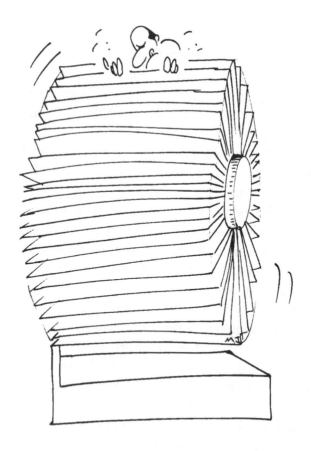

YOUR POWER IS ALMOST DIRECTLY PROPORTIONAL TO THE THICKNESS OF YOUR ROLODEX ...

job done, networking (as well as netweaving) should permeate the culture. The new corporation is a group of individuals (what some call 'teamnets') from various payrolls and enterprises (including numerous consultants) that join together for a while to produce something and then break up. In a sense organizations have always been networks, the difference being that now they tend to be flat. The spider web (closely associated with the network concept) is the best image.

In the traditional corporation, networks consisted mainly of people guided by traditional hierarchy and management control devices. No longer can purchasing managers maintain arm's length, fear-based, transaction-led relationships with suppliers. Look at the automobile manufacturers and their new relationship with a few, trusted suppliers. A US Continental Bank executive summed it up thus: 'Use best of breed, trust each other and work across boundaries. In this country we build walls and dig moats.' Project management and interdependence management involve the orchestration of a network of equals. They should become the premier corporate skills. But, you may well ask, what happens when the network disperses? 'New glue' is required to create new bases of leverage. Working in parallel with interdependence management and to abet learning over time, a knowledge management structure needs to be in place. At McKinsey and Co. the structure consists of information technology systems, a global network of internal and external experts, databased, updated and the dynamic linkages tabulated, overseen by a director of knowledge management!

As will become apparent in this voyage around the spider web, whatever your perspective, whether the CEO having to deal with outside alliances and a new breed of employee inside, a one-man-and-a-dog virtual operation with global reach or an autonomous employee, the rationale for networking is that all roads lead to knowledge. McKinsey teach their employees to first recognize what they don't know, then who and how to access to get the job done.

What is new is the intensity, a difference in kind. Workers really have to become business persons. The 'corporation' is much more ephemeral, fleeting, fickle and flat, but with an expanding and even more complex network with novel structures building centres of excellence and managing interdependence with a mix of internal and external talent. All over the world companies are decentralizing, down-sizing and forging alliances to pursue innovation. There is a balance to be struck between internal and external networking and a flexible company structure. Just look what the chief executive has to deal with, not just with the external strategy but internal culture, with less allegiance to particular companies and greater mobility (often resulting from downsizing). According to a recent MORI/DEMOS Report 'Freedom's Children' among UK 18 to 35 year olds, young people are increasingly detached, proud to be outside the system, whether corporate, political or national, although positively they are taking responsibility not only for their own values but their livelihoods. In the US more than fifty per cent of the economy is made up of small businesses, relying more than ever on self-employment supported by a community network.

A recent American study by Robert Putnam: 'Bowling Alone: America's Declining Social Capital', (heavily drawn upon by Francis Fukuyama in his book *The Social Virtues and the Creation of Prosperity*) charts the decline of civil society – a 25 per cent decline in informal socializing and 50 per cent decline in club and association membership since 1965, one key factor in the loss of what he calls 'social connectedness' being television! Fortunately, despite that worrying backdrop and the insecurity that prevails, companies and professional individuals are increasingly viewing the world through a new conceptual lens. As Marcel Proust said: 'The real art of discovery consists not in finding new lands but in seeing with new eyes.'

For companies it is the stakeholder concept (which certain politicians are attempting to broaden into civic rights and responsibilities) and for individuals too networking in a mutually reinforcing way not just to keep the wolf from the door but to lead a more fulfilling life. The philosophy of networking is win/win, not win/lose as in the excesses of 1980s capitalism.

It is quite clear that a new sense of community that exists in some part of Asia (and to which I refer later) is needed in the West. Man is a social animal, but society cannot survive based on self-interested individual interactions alone: what is required is a value-based network with a sense of purpose and governance. It is no longer about capitalism versus communism, left versus right, but a new equilibrium between individual rights and civic community, which governments alone cannot provide but which individuals and organizations involved in their local, national and increasingly regional and even global communities can. Networking is at the heart of this emerging focus on soft assets, reputation and trust centred on people and communication skills.

Now that knowledge is the company's key resource, partly thanks to restructuring and information technology, it is employees who accumulate it and have access to it, so it is they who are increasingly responsible for the company's performance. ABB, the Swiss/Swedish corporation, have recognized this, and have turned the organization into a multitude of small teams (5,000 of them) close to the sharp end.

A new relationship is being defined between the individual and the corporation. The latter provides opportunities for continued learning and skills updating in return for first-class performance, so individuals are motivated while they remain an employee and marketable when they leave. The new paradigm therefore, both for company management and individual professionals, should be the concept of the 'autonomous employee', security and fulfilment deriving from performance in a highly competitive market thanks to learning and networking. Empowerment and employability go hand in hand like the proverbial horse and carriage. It behoves top management to focus on creating an exciting work environment which binds employees, a case of continuous mutual seduction and choice, a new moral contract.

No longer the 'old boys' network' with all its imperfections that men relied on for far too long and women rebelled against with positive results, mandatory continuous performance development is the order of the day. What skills do I need to accumulate, each year for the next decade? The UK Institute of Electrical Engineers runs a points system on traditional and new skills required as an incentive and benchmark.

Keniche Ohmae in his *End of the Nation State* argues: 'Economic borders have meaning, if at all not as dividing lines between civilizations or nations but at the contours of information flow. Where information reaches, demand grows. Where demand increases the global environment has a local home.' This eloquently makes the point that if wealth creation is global, social capital and knowledge are fast becoming its leverage, requiring information gathering and contacts, not in a vacuum but in a highly focused and targeted way. To navigate your way in life requires netmapping, to decide what can be credibly and realistically cloned to expand the link of influence for the individual or the individual's organization.

Once upon a time careers were nurtured under sheltering branches of the secure corporate tree. So how do individuals now live happily ever after as a result of downsizing, greater job mobility, more small businesses, independent workers and telecommuters? Some are forming professional groups, like 'Guilds', to include personnel and career support. Sometimes it happens with people on outplacement. A group of former Penn Central executives-turned-consultants formed a guild to offer 'virtual' management teams to clients. The alliance is a *de facto* support group for members, sharing leads, referrals and problem solving. These sorts of organizations could help with purchasing, group insurance, apprenticeships, career development, office space and conference facilities. Professional associations play a similar role sharing best practice and acting as a network for jobs, information sharing and learning. The American Marketing Association, which has set up a career development role, believes people are realizing it is up to them. 'I have to do it myself. I cannot fall back on the corporation or the boss,' says Tim Prosch, Director of Marketing for the Association.

According to Sundridge Park Management Centre in the UK, British women are more stand-offish than their US counterparts but use networks to learn from their colleagues in more senior positions over long time-scales, perhaps to compensate for the lack of an old boys' network. (Of course, there is nothing to compare with the power of the US alumni groups and exclusive golf club networks, which tend to be male dominated, if less so of late.) But whereas the UK woman will hover on the fringes, the US woman will work the room, trading cards, and moving on rapidly if short-term results are not yielded. According to the research it's more a case of waiting to be introduced. This may be changing, a theme of a later chapter.

Staff who have previously held backroom positions with no responsibility for relationships are now finding they have to network both within and outside their companies. According to the Digital Equipment Company, in today's decentralized structures, the ideal firm maintains shared values working towards the same goals with high morale, and providing a backdrop for networking proper.

Professionals need to cultivate a wide range of contacts, often by-passing formal chains of command. At Siemens in Germany they recognize the broader need for their business to be part of the community and for managers to acquire interpersonal and networking skills. The boss may still be critical but it is becoming important to be seen in the right light by decision-makers inside and outside the corporation – involvement in the trade association, voluntary sectors, etc. So individual objectives and the corporate mission can often be aligned.

In my various corporate assignments I have always seen myself as a consultant because that's how I think, particularly in the communications or public relations role where the whole point is external networking, feeding back to managers the expectations of stakeholders. But this independence and objectivity was often confused with disloyalty and spending excessive amounts of time outside rather than in internal meetings. Needless to say it is a question of balance, the internal network being as vital as the external if you want to get things done.

Outside relations are important and will probably save you from being fired. Someone once said you should build bridges with friends rather than burn them with enemies, and surround your enemies with your friends. The best consultancies I know are those who invite their competitors to their annual party (competition expands the market). Now *that's* networking.

Before the Enlightenment 800 years ago, City States flourished in northern Italy thanks to the middle classes joining together to protect themselves from crime and feudalism, to help each other in good faith; this resulted in the origin of banking. This richly networked society continues to flourish today, as reflected in the shape of Italian political parties with their regional bias.

In the information age, just as a bureaucracy stamped the industrial age, hierarchy the Agrarian era and small groups roamed in Nomadic times, the network is the new signature form, moving from informal to more formal, coping with complexity. Hierarchy and bureaucracy have not been replaced, but change is now the driver and individuals need greater speed, flexibility, scope, creativity, knowledge and shared responsibility. The individual is an organization, a virtual company with scope not size. With each new set of connections in small groups we realize how connected things are, especially via the laptop, the fax and the Internet. By analogy with the term 'citizen', these denizens of the information and knowledge networks are often now called 'netizens'. It is we individuals, autonomous employees, who are shaping the future, building up lasting, not transitory relationships for mutual fulfilment and achievement.

Success in the twenty-first century requires an understanding that the world is very personal and accessible, the trick being to take control of destiny working with others. Links are at the heart of networks, connective tissue extending in every direction and joining people across distance and time. The future will be characterized by multiple, overlap teams forming horizontal corporations and virtual enterprises – flexible, richly connected and with high levels of trust.

With the tremendous pace of change and interdependence, it is now impossible to get the job done quick enough, achieve things with an optimum mix of information on where to base decisions simply via traditional structures and organizations. The spider's web is the only way; but what a tangled web we weave.

2 The Tangled Web We Weave

'Power is shifting out from under those with a formal
position towards those with authority based on
knowledge and certain psychological/political skills.'   Alvin Toffler

'Manage your future or someone else will.'   Peter Drucker

A recent analysis of twenty futurists reveals some common patterns – political instability, the shrinking planet, population growth leading to the break-up of the homogenous society, multi-cultural, multi-choice with neither the small pastoral model of society prevailing nor 'big is beautiful', rather one in the other, termed the 'mosaic society'. Questions of authority, political leadership, information overload, insecurity, inward communities 'cocooning' will vie with global interconnectedness, cutting a swathe across communities, requiring a 'polymath' mentality. Now we have networks, groups working across boundaries of all kinds as knowledge replaces muscle and machine as the new source of wealth and social capital.

The information revolution creates 'One thousand points of light embracing the entire culture, where power and creativity are dispersed, decentralized and democratized', according to Ray Smith, CEO Bell Atlantic Inc. In a network you connect up, down, out and around and instead of a few hundred names in the Rolodex you should now have many thousands. Networking allows you to build on what you have: it is empowering. Individuals, like companies, must now align their personal objectives and values with their tactical networking. This will more and more be global, between companies and industries and within industries at a local level, California being a classic example in the film and computer industries.

With tougher competition facing limits to growth, organizations will reach optimal size, seeking qualitative development rather than quantitative growth, focusing on alliances with people as the key. Networks are called for when scope is large but size is small. This is also true of the closer relationship between the sales sharp end and the customer, leading to the development of 'relationship marketing'.

In the new era, the networking principle of 'unifying purpose' plays the same role as goal specialization does in bureaucracy. The focus on purpose in a network is more intense because it is the primary source of legitimacy and holds people together voluntarily. Relationships develop over time with technology providing new options for interaction, enabling new constellations to form. If we can communicate with anyone, anywhere, anytime, our networks should expand. A pre-requisite however is to have a goal, a plan, a mission, based on your value system. The networking tactic used to help achieve that end-game should ideally start now rather than when you need it. As has already happened in the US, UK high-street retailers are finally realizing that they must network to stay in business in the face of shopping mall competition. They must network with each other, with politicians and local authorities, with community interest groups, as well as retain and grow the customer base.

The nuclear industry, while a set of individual companies (some state, some privatized), which function within national energy policies and health and safety regulations, has realized that the issues facing it are global, that whereas Germany may be contracting, China is expanding. It is vital for them to work together as a group of individuals via company alliances and industry association partnerships spanning the globe, networking not only together to share best practice but to develop a network globally of those (say) 3,000 people they wish to influence and who have an influence over their future. With governments and pressure groups interested primarily in the immediate TV 'soundbite' on policy for the next election and the nuclear industry interested in its global business and licence to operate long term, research is necessary to identify those 'think-tanks' with whom they can dialogue in order to at least influence the longer-term thinking.

Those nations such as China, Japan, Korea which are currently promoting new nuclear programmes all recognize the benefits of international networking to ensure international standards and to share knowledge, whether about technology or public opinion. Significantly the first global network set up by the nuclear industry was the World Association of Nuclear Operators (WANO) in the aftermath of the Chernobyl accident in the former Soviet Union a decade ago.

The nuclear industry is a large and global industry, but as Eastman Chemical Company's CEO told *Business Week*, 'Our organization chart looks like a pizza with a lot of pepperoni sitting on it.' In other words cor-

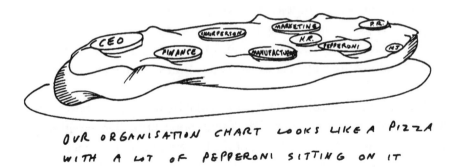

OUR ORGANISATION CHART LOOKS LIKE A PIZZA
WITH A LOT OF PEPPERONI SITTING ON IT

porate organization charts are just the sum totals of overlapping circles held together by horizontal and vertical networking.

But just as there are different types of corporate networks such as the economic megagroups in Silicon Valley, or the Keiretsu in Japan, the Alliances of Motorola and Apple, the Enterprise networks focusing on internal markets as in the case of ABB and Eastman or as the more team-orientated approaches of AT&T, so too can individuals (and small businesses) form different shapes and sizes of networks. As British Institute of Directors' David Treadwell says, 'Regardless of your box, the net is interconnected, you just have tap into it.' Interestingly the Institute of Directors prepares a conference delegate network book for its conferences with details of each delegate, their organization and how to reach them.

To solve problems and achieve goals in this diverse, complex, interdependent world will require the formation of new networks involving all proactive people on the planet. Networking is about building relationships, to exchange information and build lasting customers, clients, partners, alliances, colleagues and friends. I don't waste energy creating enemies, because the best revenge comes from sitting on the river's edge watching the bodies floating by.

According to David Clutterbuck, the management writer and co-author of *The Winning Streak*, young managers should seize ownership of their careers earlier in life if they intend to reach the top. 'Whereas in the past it was possible to plot a career course across a medium-weather sea, now it's more like shooting white-water rapids in a rubber dinghy', a Kinsley Lord report 'Routes to the Top', co-written by Clutterbuck states.

Of course there is natural networking that we all do every day. But standing at the bar waiting for people to come up to you is passive. Even attending a conference and benefiting from the networking it throws up is not true networking, unless you've pre-selected the conference as appropriate to goals set, the key people pursued at the conference and followed up later. When you land a job do you always write to those who helped you along the way? As we all know, times change and nothing lasts for ever.

This is the age of collaborative individualism which is best suited to someone with the following profile: autonomous, proactive, creative, politically skilled, articulate, a listener, ethical, empathic and iconoclastic.

Bringing together the changing nature of individual professionals' lives and the approaches of organizations, some writers refer to the open systems approach of the 1970s being replaced by the collaborative approach, organized around small, loosely-coupled units, which leads to collaborative individualism, whether that individual remains inside a company or is self-employed. Now that employees have access to information plus knowledge, an essential management goal, they assert, is to facilitate collaboration and the brokering of strategic partnerships, the new paradigm being self-fulfilment for the individual and global competitiveness for the firm.

With discontinuous change, when the lessons of history cannot be learned, individuals must rely on building and nurturing networks for information sharing and support. Professionals now must 'network big'. At the micro, personal level individual professionals, just like their corporate counterparts, should use networking to enable them to concentrate on what they do best, while contracting out to allies. Networking fosters innovation and access to global opportunities.

The more firms can train their managers to think long term, deal with soft issues such as vision, equity and relationships, to look outwards rather than constantly refer to 'We in the company', the more they are empowered, despite the risks to corporate cohesion. The more they are tutored to recognize that the soft issues are now hard core, the better equipped individuals will be for the tough world outside that is either forced upon them or they choose for lifestyle reasons. It's a significant paradox that despite the growth of head-to-head global competition between nations and firms, it's not necessarily those which cut costs rather than invest in people or which look solely to the bottom line rather than building relationships which succeed.

In his *Post-Capitalist Society*, Peter Drucker, the management guru looking into his crystal ball, sees a society of loose organizations and networks with less domination by nation states giving way to global but also tribal connections.

Another guru, Charles Handy, believes in 'upside-down thinking'. By the twenty-first century less than fifty per cent of the workforce will be in conventional, full-time jobs, forcing a rethink of the work, job, career notions with higher-order intelligence skills needed, pressure on the educational system for lifelong learning, a key element of networking. Older people, long ago thrown onto the scrap heap will, with wisdom, a wish to contribute, and living longer, return to the workforce, needing to acquire a new network and tap into the old one they haven't left properly greased, and in need of repair.

There's a pressure on women to enter and re-enter the workforce, and now that the glass ceiling is gradually being shattered, a greater competitiveness on the part of women to learn the art of networking. A recent report from the UK Equal Opportunities Commission reveals more complaints from men about sex discrimination. One journalist quipped that female talents equip them 'beautifully for the new age of brief contracts'.

It is not my experience that, as Tim Heald says, 'Networking, like sex, is one of the few activities at which a gifted and enthusiastic amateur has a built-in advantage over the purely professional.' This has been the approach of men through the ages via the old boys network. Women are more attuned to the new soft skills, more self-employed, sensitive to the more informal, horizontal networks within organizations and communities and are more flexible. Women need to cultivate mentors, engage in training, foster professionals and social contacts and are generally more proficient at it. This is certainly the case in the public relations industry on both sides of the Atlantic. In my younger days I dated a public relations woman in New York in the normal way men do. Ten years on I visited her and she was so busy tending to her hundred staff (mostly women) that we had to eat lunch at her desk! It also applies to the other service and information industries too. Doing deals runs counter to the value systems of many women. Transactions-orientation is the antithesis of networking. Sadly for the more extreme feminists, although women must work extra hard to achieve success, the best involve men in the process.

Susan Bloch, a career consultant, believes 'A well-developed network of contacts is vital for the effective marketing of *Me* plc.' Irene Harris founded 'Network' in 1981 for women in middle management and another just called 'Club 2000' for those in senior management because having run

Women of the Year lunches she found there was a need for women to meet more than once a year. She explains that women are often isolated in what they do and feel a need to meet other women in different positions. She believes networking is about building a circle of contacts, very fluid but which goes on for ever. As women become more accustomed to networking, the need for such formal monthly lunches may dissolve: but the networks will remain. She warns that junior women often don't feel the same need, but it is important to start young, not only to broaden the outlook but to build social capital for the time when it may be needed at a more senior level.

This author suspects it was the failure of traditional men's clubs in London to allow women to join which prompted her to set up the network. Equally there are the 'looser' but just as important 'Ladies who lunch' networks in London and New York, Cannes and Palm Beach, formed to share social gossip but also to provide support, just as the professional ones do. 'If architecture is frozen mosaic, then social networks are frozen gossip' said Paul Barker in *Guardian Weekly*.

On a variation of theme, Stephanie Lynn's Businesswomen's Network founded in 1992 has been extended to a Businessmen's Network to encourage top men to meet women in similar positions so as to share ideas and experiences. This is a very formal network and all are interviewed first. Interestingly, on setting up the group she tried hard to find an alternative word to describe the process but kept it because, while overused, it conjures up an appropriate image. Her view is that it is ultimately about trust and social support (each member gives one hour free advice), but it is not about selling. She believes women are much better at diversifying than men but pull themselves up much quicker than men after adversity, although they need teaching how to network. But once they do, the men should watch out, as experience shows (including my own).

So people are moving jobs more, changing careers, working harder with greater stress and insecurity, becoming more independent, retiring earlier. But whereas continuous learning and networking is a challenge, we all have a chance to shape our work to suit our lives. The portfolio life (coined by Charles Handy) of coursework, study, contribution, free work and salaried work gives everyone an opportunity to gain meaning, make a contribution and meet new people for fulfilment, to achieve 'personal growth'. Of course this can and often does lead to a clash between hierarchy and networks. But if corporate cultures promote networking for motivational reasons, the driving forces of trust, excitement, innovation and personal enquiry can be a competitive weapon for sustainable success. These approaches can be used for remedying organizational problems, consciousness raising on global issues, building coalitions, galvanizing professional societies and fuelling a consulting resource.

All the recent spate of management books when referring to the globalization of the economy, importance of knowledge as a source of value added plus the crucial role of information technology and communications cite *self-employment, teamwork* and *networking* as crucial ingredients.

In his seminal book *The Work of Nations, Preparing Ourselves for 21st Century Capitalism*, Robert Reich talks of a nation's economic performance being inextricably linked to the knowledge and skills its people can bring to various international webs. These people he calls 'Symbolic analysts', the 'Netweavers', generally those in public relations and advertising, management consulting and entertainment (four fields in which this writer has been privileged to work) who identify problems, solve problems, facilitate via representation and referral, acting as strategic brokers, a great phrase for someone who pulls together the right people to think, act creatively, get the job done. It's interesting though that some of these great networking professions now find it necessary to use headhunters to recruit on their behalf, because they realize that their networking is insufficiently systematic.

Talking of headhunting, a field with which I've always been fascinated, it's interesting how the bad ones are indiscreet and the good ones recognize they have to give selected information to gain some. While they must nurture their clients, even some of the candidates they reject should be nurtured too; for who knows where they may end up!

Networking then is a way to the art of discovering patterns in the world, making sense of otherwise unrelated facts, making useful connections. It's about weaving new options into our safety nets! With job insecurity remaining the number one concern in the West and the 'feel ghastly' factor at work showing no sign of lifting, this becomes even more imperative. With one out of two not working after the age of 55 and the trend continuing, older people will need to brush up on their network structure and linkages.

Given that the best networking begins if one is already in a network, a start-up should have a general focus, not a specific goal. It should not, at least at the outset, be institutionalized, lest it become fossilized. Later you can organize a newsletter, a central secretariat and publish a list of members.

To design a network requires a purpose. So make an inventory of your personal 'ego-net' and 'positional net'. Marry up your strengths and interests with demand. Add your material assets in terms of, for example, club memberships. What are the resource gaps? Do desk research to ascertain the network nodes and linkages. Assess those you know. Are they people of influence – 'stars'? Are they 'gatekeepers' or 'boundary spanners'? How is your network structured (is it transactional or attribute driven) and what is your normal network style?

This is not gobbledegook; just marketing and management jargon for a natural process which has to be put on a rigorous footing and have some intellectual coherence if the seeds sown are to reap the rewards. Where to begin? In the words of Dr Stephen Covey, 'First things first' and 'Do it now!'

3 The Law of Ten

'Ignorance is bliss in a quotation but folly in a career.'

The *Economist* Poster Ad

'90 per cent of life is showing up.'

Woody Allen

Marilyn Monroe is reputed to have said, 'I've been a calendar, but I've never been on time.' By quoting this, and also that great comedian Woody Allen I suggest that while networking is not the be-all and end-all of life, it sure helps; that in networking it's the little things, the small touches that count. *That's the first law.*

I referred earlier to those who don't return phone calls. It's the simplest aspect of networking, to respond to people. It's not even proactive. That phone call which breaks into your single-minded, too-busy-to-be-disturbed day, could ultimately turn out to be your life-line, even though you don't know it at the moment (otherwise you'd return the call). It's not as though you must do it now. Why not pile them up, certainly put them in order of importance. But do it sooner rather than later, for in any culture, certainly in the West, it's downright rude. Even the most successful people should remember this, however busy and shielded from callers. A few of the most successful answer their own calls. Get to know the gatekeepers, the PA to the Chairman or head of the private office. Networkers are so keen on getting to the top, they tend to forget the little people who know where the bodies are buried, for they are almost as powerful. I know someone, highly successful, who only returns calls if they're clients, prospects or girl-friends! There are always excuses and rationalizations, always confusions between the short and the long term, the immediate and distant contact, the urgent and the potentially important. It all depends on your goals and value systems. The other side of the coin is: if you promise to do something, do it. Too many people over-promise! 'I'll get back to you', 'Let's have lunch soon', 'I'll introduce you to so and so'. Why not just be honest and say 'Don't call me, I'll call you'!

Other little touches, so long as they are sincere and perceived to be are

CATCHING UP ON THOSE PHONE MESSAGES

to write personal notes in the Christmas card, tailored to that individual. There is one remarkable UK company Chairman who does this to great effect and with little effort. It's a great annual mail-shot, a key element in anyone's networking, an investment in time and keeping those databases up to date. But it must be sincere. Of course discard extinct cards (defined as 'I can't remember who they are' three years later).

Which brings me to the *second law*. On the assumption spelt out earlier that you need a larger overlapping series of networks than ever these days, success is predicated not just on the size of that Rolodex but its quality. So not only is it vital to keep the lists cleansed but notes kept on where you met them, through whom and who they know as well as what the mutual interest is. The typical professional should have 3,500 contacts (direct and indirect). They should be catalogued by 'Who', 'Type', 'Criticality', prioritized into 'Invest', 'Hold' and 'Divest'.

Just as when you go into an interview with an investigative journalist you even up the odds by learning as much about the person ahead of time, it is important to make profile notes, particularly as your network extends and it's impossible to remember. This is particularly important during a long trip, especially if the networks are overlapping. Writing on the cards is a good start.

It always amazes me how some in public relations whose business is making the connections, fail to do their research not just on those connections and what they think of the client or organization, but who they influence and who influences them. In the financial community for example, journalists are influenced by their peer group as much as by their sources and those sources' sources, whether they be buy- or sell-side analysts who influence each other and in turn are influenced by the journalists' perspective. This dynamic is rarely put into context so that those who need to know understand the nature of the network. The same parallel exists in the political lobbying field whether in London, Washington or Brussels.

Doing business in Asia for a Westerner is tough, particularly in China. The complex web that exists for example between the Beijing government and the regional authorities, between the politicians and the officials, between the bureaucracy and the institutes that control most industries and the interlocking nature of those organizations, when overlaid on the new breed of autonomous entrepreneurs particularly in the south of the country and especially away from the capital, makes it imperative that the network is understood and shared between individuals and Western companies doing business there: that nothing can be done without co-operation. In the current chaos in Russia with official decision-making paralyzed because institutions' cogs don't overlap, it's vital to put together networks to ensure the right levers are pressed. Even then, as ABB CEO Percy Barnevik warns, 'Stay away from fast people intent on a fast buck. Go for young champions rather than traditional top managers.' It gives new meaning to Russian roulette.

The third law, also applicable to operating in China but a universal law of networking, is its long-term nature based on trusting relationships. It also shocks one how many people are indiscreet. This betrays trusts, destroys the mutuality of networking. Dr Steven Covey says 'If there's little or no trust, there is no foundation for permanent success.' The deal-making/

transactions 1980s are over, having been replaced by the need for long-term relationships, partnerships and alliances, individual and corporate.

Currently, more networks break up than are created, but *real* networking, if it is to result in a more fulfilling career and lifestyle, is about investment, giving as well as receiving. A bad networker assumes that it is a one-way street, so is totally focused on a single issue or intent.

My former boss at PA Consulting Group, Kep Simpson, who finds it hard to analyze the subject, nevertheless believes networking to be about relationships. If relationships are based on respect, he argues, this requires a willingness to be involved by each member of the network. The essence of networking is what you put into it. This is the *fourth law,* that repeated interaction rather than pursuit of an immediate pay-back encourages co-operation based on mutual trust.

I'm privileged to belong to one of the best networks in the world of public relations, which despite its limited resources and specific focus has partnerships far wider than that profession, in politics, environment and education as well as the business community, thus punching above its weight in over twenty countries. It's called the International Public Relations Association (IPRA). Several presidents over the years have lost their jobs because of their commitment to it, through lack of understanding of its network nexus at the crossroads of influence and information of interest to the organization that particular president worked for. I was more fortunate in that regard, because when I was most active my employers, the top US PR firm Burson-Marsteller, viewed it as seamless to their goals and aspirations. The IPRA network has helped my partner and me in building up a small business to become the only truly international company in its sector, Carma International.

On a personal level, apart from the learning process, it has been the most rewarding network of my life; yet so many won't join because they're not joiners, but others always ask what's in it for them. How short sighted and short term, not to mention what it says about them as people. I well remember a decade ago a famous New York PR guru accusing IPRA of being too linked to the irrelevant 'developing world'. He's had to eat his words as he's now one of the top firms in China. Outside the traditional Western capitals, places like Malaysia and India are now the fastest-growing PR markets.

The *fifth law* is to think ahead. It has been referred to earlier in this book, but it bears repetition. Build up equity, goodwill, social capital *before* you need it. It is amazing how people in top positions – ministers, chief executives and show-business stars fail to network once they sit on the pinnacle of power, cocooning themselves, surrounded by sycophants. When they fall to earth when forced from power or lose their lustre they've very little to fall back on. It's partly arrogance but chiefly lack of planning.

When I joined Ford Motor Company, with the biggest budget I'd ever had to spend to that point (and since), I received a most odd letter from a consultant whom I vaguely remembered but who seemed to know me well, having, he wrote, 'watched my remarkable career progression with considerable interest'. The same happened to a colleague in New York who had just moved into an exalted position on the client side after a lifetime in consultancy. He received a similar note from a top consultant who should know better. Even though my colleague knew this person by repute, they'd hardly, if ever met and his reputation plummeted on receipt. Where were the notes during all the intervening years?

Letters are terrific mail-shots if not out of the blue. The Chairman of a large public-relations consultancy built the early part of his career by sending notes to people when he saw them mentioned or picking out press cuttings of interest as a peg to make an introduction. But he did it consistently to key targets and potential targets rather than in a once-in-a-lifetime manner which gets noticed by its very chutzpah. But it hardly adds to the stock of social capital. Another top consultant always writes to people he likes or respects when they change or lose their jobs to genuinely try and keep them. This obviously places him in a good position for future business.

The *sixth law* is to network in informal situations, when there is no pressure or obligation, at a sporting or civil reception pre-screened by you for its relevance. Networking requires some of the same skills as selling but has more of the characteristics of marketing – more informal, more indirect, less obvious – according to Reginald Watts, a leading strategic communications consultant and former co-author with me. It just means in seeking out opportunities for this kind of setting, ensure that they are appropriate to your objectives.

Jayne Mitchell, a career management consultant, warns of the dangers of networking with friends at least for business purposes. This is why the setting is important. A dinner party at a friend's house is different from a networking lunch or a telephone call at business.

The *seventh law* is to recognize that the person most likely to give you the crucial lead is unlikely to be someone you know well and who talks with you often. The most useful contacts are weak connections and are likely to be those with a vast armoury of contacts. This is vital if you're attempting to move to the wider circle beyond your immediate 'sphere of influence'. These are likely to be the least accessible of people on first observation, simply by their seniority. It's therefore important either to become known yourself via a speech or article, which can be on a narrow subject (we're not talking here of intense media scrutiny of the kind enjoyed by movie stars and Royals). It could be that you can dangle some information before this person that is useful to them, which is equal trading. More likely, however, the approach should be by someone known to both parties – hence the real size of your network reaches well beyond those you know. Third-party endorsement is more credible than you telling the intended target how good you or your company are.

So live up to expectations (because expectation shortfall is disproportionate). Networking is about listening, it's about not being afraid to ask questions. A good networker is flattered, curious, likes to chat, loves to be at the centre of information and gossip, use phrases such as 'Assume I know nothing, tell me all' and 'If you won't help can you recommend anyone that can?' Be prepared to give as well as to receive, to reciprocate. Ultimately networking is about bridging the gaps between those you know and those you need to or would like to. But the point of departure is what do I need to reach my goal, or live up to my values on the more day-to-day level, how can I find out what I need to know, who is likely to have the information? Having said that, everyone is busy so be precise and just ask one or two questions. This is useful for those seeking a job or changing function within a company.

It's always said that *who* you know is vital and *what* you know helps. Nowadays *when* you know can make or break a situation. The *eighth law* is to build a broad and deep range of relationships. Every time you add a single direct contact you exploit your indirect, linking people from a spider-web structure that catches lots of information from diverse sources on the 'six degrees of separation' principle, strong ties, weak ties. To manage a complex role you need to piece together informal, unrelated bits of information. It's impossible to stay in the know with a few or narrow sets of contacts. Increasingly it's as important to have the total picture as it is to have specialist knowledge. Zig-zag career paths in that sense are preferable to vertical ones, as are cross-functional, bridge-building groups. It's important to hang out in the marketplace beyond the confines of the local community, the discipline or company. Hence the importance of chambers of commerce and trade associations, whose function is information, contact and leveraging the network. Lift your eyes from the immediate task and extend beyond your immediate circles. I accept it requires courage, but even up the odds with preparation. It's worth the investment – you can have lunch with a friend or colleague any day. Apart from all the new people I have to meet ritualistically on the circuit, I try to meet someone each week who expands either my personal or professional network.

The *ninth law*, building on all the elements above because it is an integrated system, is certainly to jump-start a network if you're unused to the process for the short term, but in parallel ensure you invest in a longer-term strategic approach to defining the strengths and weaknesses of it, defining your spheres of influence, networking notables etc. This is about targeting. Keep at it and be systematic, staying in touch several times a year in different ways. Especially if it's a start-up business it has to be co-ordinated and consistent to be credible. Realize that networking is part of a broader lifestyle and communications approach to personal goals or the organization's mission. How this applies to small firms, particularly service firms, will be dealt with in a separate chapter.

Finally, in order to become a role model of networking – a 'networking notable', which in turn helps you stay in the swim – it is vital to stay in circulation. A friend of mine lost his livelihood and as a result his confidence and dignity. I told him he needed to be seen at his club and lunch strategically with those who could help him in a potentially new role. His story has a happy ending, because he took a deep breath, decided what was important and networked with a passion.

That's the *tenth law*. Networking is an attitude to life, about ways of behaving, about growth just as much as it is a marketing and targeting process. A philosophy exists behind the tactics, important as they are to get right.

Perhaps it is after all about 'enlightened serendipity', as Kep Simpson defines it, working hard to bring about coincidence, streams of consciousness, chance meetings, making two and two add value to five.

An inside job – key traits of a good networker

Goals:	Big goals.
Enjoy it:	If it isn't fun, it isn't worth it.
Confidence:	Positive mental attitude.
Integrity:	Win/win.
Work:	90 per cent of success is effort.
Risk:	Take risks, learn by mistakes and be proactive.
Communicate and contribute:	Ask for help but lend a hand; also say 'Thank you.'
People:	Part of a team, surround yourself with good people.
Energy:	High octane levels essential.

4 Network Organizations: Concepts and Cases

'And they that weave networks shall be confounded.'

Isaiah, Old Testament

'Enterprise web.'

Robert Reich

Davos, in Switzerland, is best known as an exclusive ski resort, except for one week a year when the town hosts the world's most powerful network jamboree – the World Economic Forum.

Each year over a thousand chief executives from many countries, embracing different sectors, ascend the mountain to listen to, debate with and have contact dinners among the leading academics, national politicians and heads of international governmental organizations on a variety of global, geographic and sectoral themes and issues ranging from 'Challenges beyond growth' to 'The coming of the global information society: nations or networks', from 'Teledemocracy' to 'Tomorrow's company'.

The business and social programme is organized in such a way that given the choice of speakers, subject areas and social events, where you rub shoulders with the good and the great, you need a Doctorate to sort it all out. And if that doesn't blow your mind – it's rather like compressing a term at college into three days – then the elaborate IT system allows delegates to access everyone present at the meeting to arrange for further networking in the hour before dinner. That is if you are not in desperate need of a nap!

Throughout the year members of this Swiss-run, exclusive club, depending on the Issue, Information and Interface category, meet up in industry-sector groups from energy to telecommunications, or a small-business section, or the young entrepreneurs group.

I was privileged to be part of a WEF 100-business-person delegation from twenty countries visiting the Mekong Delta Sub-region comprising six countries including Thailand and Vietnam and held in Hanoi. Apart from detailed briefings from government ministers and experts, we spent time with regional heads of foreign banks, law firms and research companies with practical knowledge about the issues facing, and information on the region.

An innovation is to hold an industry summit (at the University of Chicago in 1996) at which business leaders in small-group sessions share the latest knowledge in technology and management, discuss the key strategic issues facing industry sectors with academics and consulting firms, as well as mix with representatives from a network of global companies to assess their specific challenges. Another WEF initiative is the Global Leaders of Tomorrow group, who share their specific expertise at the summit, which is reinforced by a multi-media Intranet system, integrating the top decision-makers around the world into a World Electronic Community, 'WELCOM'.

So the WEF is a unique organization founded by Klaus Schwab for 'a more peaceful world' but in practice designed to build bridges across frontiers, and to share ideas on horizontal and vertical issues requiring resolution between the business/political divide. The point is that it is *issue*-, *information*-, *interface*-driven, ultimately leading to Influence, the *raison d'être* of networking.

One of the subjects most often debated at the WEF annual meeting is sustainable development and the role that the private sector must increasingly play alongside host governments, particularly in emerging economies, in obtaining a balance between growth and conservation.

A new actor in the field is the non-governmental organization. The Prince of Wales Business Leaders' Forum, founded by HRH Prince Charles but with policy driven by an international board of directors from international companies in the UK, US, Japan and Germany is one such organization. It has adopted a single-issue, environment-sustainable development (and good corporate citizenship) and since its inception just over five years ago has made tremendous progress in developing partnerships to achieve practical goals, most notably in emerging countries such as China, Central Europe, Russia, South Africa, India and Mexico.

The PWBLF has an 'International Partnership Network', an informal association of 'partnership practitioners', the objective of which is a task force on sustainable development designed to share examples of best practice, publicize success stories, exchange people, review strategy, and lobby jointly.

While many of those linked to the IPN come from NGOS and cross-sector umbrella organizations, increasingly they are being joined by key representatives from business, the media, academics, bilateral aid agencies, and local and national governments. It was agreed that the programme would focus on 'the encouragement of regional networks based around specific themes and the exchange of experience'.

Building on its experience demonstrating the role business can play as partners in development, the PWBLF has initiated the Global IT Partnership, the aim of which is to work with business, NGOs, international agencies and local communities to mobilize IT to the benefit of social, environmental and economic progress, acting as a catalyst for projects to ensure that poor people are not excluded from the opportunities afforded by the information revolution. It collaborates with partners such as the 'Globe' Programme (an international environmental education and science partnership, as linking students, teachers and scientists in studying the global environment).

The PWBLF Partner network is developing a library on the Internet focusing on business and stakeholder partnerships for sustainable development. Regional organizations include the St Petersburg Partnership Initiative, Bulgaria Development Programme and Shanghai Business Leadership Programme.

Finally, the Partners in Development Programme, a joint initiative between the PWBLF and the World Bank Group, undertakes video conferences to exchange information and experiences, produces research and publications and undertakes projects to demonstrate how public–private sector partnerships can tackle specific challenges. The first was a partnership between BP, the World Bank, the Colombian government and local communities in the Casanare region of Colombia.

The point about this example is to illustrate how a small organization with an enthusiastic but limited staff can quite literally 'punch above its weight' via international partnerships, pulling together groups and organizations to achieve success on a global issue at regional, national and local levels.

With the private sector having the technology and increasingly the capital, not to mention human resources, and the developed world holding the knowledge and the emerging markets or economies needing it, particularly in the energy, environment, economics trade-offs given burgeoning populations, it's amazing what small organizations via networking can pull off when an issue, information (knowledge) sharing and interfaces (via alliances and partnerships) are aligned to achieve influence. This doesn't in any way underestimate the catalytic role played by the Prince of Wales himself at the apex of the network. The Royal Institute of International Affairs (Chatham House) in London aims to spot international developments just as business people feel they need an injection of special expertise. The Chatham House formula is to use its extensive contacts to provide top-level expertise. How do the 2,700 delegates per year benefit? From jobs, checking up on what the competition is doing, or just for networking; in my experience it is a remarkable bridge-building exercise between the political and business world.

The European Community Committee of the American Chamber of Commerce in Belgium has forged strong relationships with European and US business interest organizations and co-ordinates EC affairs for the European Council of American Chambers of Commerce, representing sixteen chambers of commerce in Europe.

The EC Committee is a member of the US Industrial Co-ordinating Group which co-ordinates the main American business organizations, comprising the US Chamber of Commerce and other US bodies. The EC Committee also maintains close contacts with other representative bodies centred on European Union Affairs such as UNICE (the European Federation of Employers) and the European Round Table of Industrialists (ERT) founded by two former Chairmen of Volvo Sweden and Philips of the Netherlands to cut a swathe across divergent national policies on such issues as European transport infrastructure.

Even the European Commission, a complex bureaucracy, in its attempt to remove barriers to trade in the single market, has set up a network of 1,200 contact points around the member states to sort out issues informally. So if your company or you as an individual based in Brussels are interested in having influence on this issue, sharing information, then this would be a unique interface. All it takes is a little research and contact-building, then investing the time (and a little money) to become involved. But few smaller companies or individuals, especially autonomous employees, bother to take that extra leap to expand their sphere of influence by joining this kind of network with regional and global tentacles.

The organization for which I serve as Director-General, the British Nuclear Industry Forum, is a company, has membership reserved exclusively for companies in that particular sector and undertakes activities that are expected of a lobbying and trade association. But ultimately, as regular member surveys attest, the organization is a 'virtual network'. With a relatively small staff, about the size of a medium consultancy, its role is to deal with the global issues, inputting and outputting information, interfacing with a whole range of stakeholders from pressure groups to politicians, opponents to supporters from Sellafield to Shanghai, all for one reason – to influence public opinion and opinion formers via leveraging the network. This is achieved by a whole host of techniques using a variety of channels of communication, including, importantly, third-party advocacy. But a vital ingredient is to build a database of stakeholders with whom to hold a dialogue on a regular basis, including building alliances with those (such as the insurance profession) sharing similar issues to the nuclear industry on global warming/climate change, not to mention partnership with similar fora in other countries such as the US and Japan. As has been discussed elsewhere, if nuclear energy is part of a global, long-term issue it is critical to identify and become involved with a variety of international organizations as a way of expanding the network, exchanging information and seeking influence on this issue.

Of course, like a lot of industries such as computer software with its 'IT Clubs', the nuclear industry has a range of international networks, some more formal than others, to exchange best practice (on, for example, safety/technology), track the issues, analyze the dynamics of influence and disseminate information.

Another network to which I have been privileged to belong, referred to earlier, is the International Public Relations Association, comprising about 1,200 senior practitioners in many countries. It's a veritable United Nations, which I call 'a network with soul', because apart from the learning experience and business contacts it's been a source of lasting friendships and a paradigm whereby one sees the world in its entirety rather than from the perspective of a particular country or sector. I am amazed at how many people who join committees can only see the issue or industry from their national or corporate perspective. Whenever I travel to IPRA's meetings or take part in one or more of their numerous working parties, the hotel is always full of the Global Dental Convention or the Concrete Manufacturers Association. All these organizations have their ups and downs depending on the current leadership, economic vicissitudes and other competing attractions. But apart from constantly replenishing the membership with younger enthusiasts representative of the world profession, IPRA has found that building partnerships with the business community, academia, international governmental and non-governmental organizations, the diplomatic community and the media to be particularly beneficial. But not in a vacuum, in a focused way concentrating on a few key issues. That's the way to limit the number of people you need to access, and optimizes the information flow so that influence can be maximized.

It matters not whether you're a self-employed or employed individual changing functions or careers, a small or large company, with a traditional structure or a virtual one, in a local community or global. The key to achieving sustainable networking success is the alignment of:

ISSUES – INFORMATION – INTERFACES = INFLUENCE.

Put another way:

WHY – WHAT – WHO = WIN/WIN.

This is called the matrix methodology which places networking and networks onto a conceptual framework. Yet how many people, like rehearsing for a speech, leave it till the last minute or don't invest the time to get it right. A little effort to define those issues you or your company are concerned about, and therefore the information you hold or lack leading to those contacts (individuals or organizations) you know or need can result in positive influence out of all proportion to the inputs.

Whilst successful, sustainable networking is largely a product of a pro-active management approach, born of a vision, objectives and a value-system, there is clearly a range of practical guidelines that, linked and locked together, deliver an effective programme. Essentially a networking programme divides into four key activities: audit, target, promote, cultivate.

Audit

Find out how you are currently perceived versus how you wish to be, and plan a campaign to narrow the gap. *Plot* your immediate spheres of influence and connections, in turn plotting their spheres of influence and connections. *Identify* the barriers to wider influence (internal and external) and assess how to remove or at least overcome them. The Pareto principle states that most people spend 80 per cent of their time on less important matters when if they concentrated on the 20 per cent important they could solve most things. *Plan* a programme of reaching a wider circle, infiltrating wheels within wheels. *Remember* you have to be a member of a group to influence another.

Target

Consider who/what should be your network and why. *Research* their agendas and interests (business, political and personal). *Identify* their circle of contacts and connections. *Inform* yourself about what is going on and who is doing it. When you're off to a gathering for the first time, even up the odds by knowing as much as you can about what goes on and who goes. When you get there study the delegates list during the speeches!

Promote

Network yourself or your organization (or both) through events, receptions, join suitable partnership and membership organizations. A number of informal luncheon clubs as well as the more structured network organizations or those you need to lobby have been referred to in this book, not least the rise of women's groups. *Publish* results, achievements and circulate them to chosen targets as has been discussed in the chapter on marketing the small business. *Empower* yourself by mixing among the decision makers. *Campaign* with the media.

Cultivate

Make good use of networking notables or third-party advocates once you've got them, yet without becoming a burden. *Appreciate* the support of advocates by letting them know how they have helped. *Seek* partnership opportunities with them and their organizations and *inform* them about your successes, achievements and future plans via newsletters.

The Duchess of Windsor once said 'One can never be too thin or too rich.' Today she might have been more on target had she added 'One can never have too many people in one's network'! The *issues* must be clear, the *information* parameters set and the *interfaces* listed by category and annotated with their interconnectedness. Then your and your company's network will become advocates working on your behalf, and you and your organization will achieve *influence*. Networks truly work for you when you are resting and playing!

NETWORKS TRULY WORK FOR YOU
WHEN YOU ARE RESTING AND PLAYING

Professor Tim Traverse-Healy, no mean networker himself and a long-time mentor for me, has said, 'In an interdependent world, information is power when acted upon.' He also said, 'If controversy is the price of democracy, dialogue is the currency of contact.'

Matrix methodology

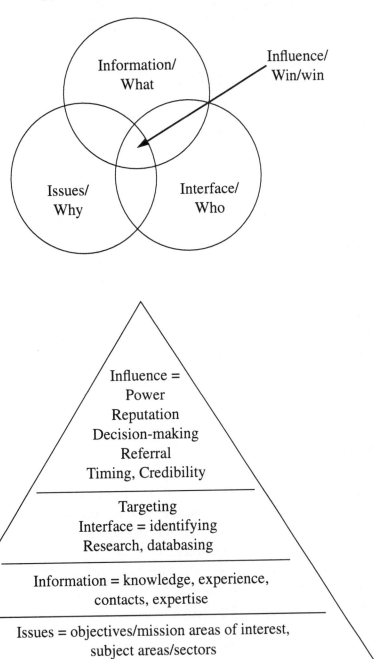

5 Bamboo Networking: Overseas Chinese Model

'Countries don't trade, people and businesses do.
Networks are at the core of the new global economy.'

John Naisbitt, MegaTrends Asia

'The overseas Chinese are a network of networkers.'

John Naisbitt, MegaTrends Asia

They make up less than ten per cent of the population of south-east Asia yet the overseas Chinese/ethnic Chinese living outside China drive much of the region's business, controlling up to two-thirds of the retail trade, providing nine out of ten of its billionaires and have overtaken the Japanese (in crisis themselves) as its primary source of capital.

Guanxi (connections) is the chief reason given for the success of the fifty million ethnic Chinese worldwide. Though by no means a homogenous group, they have largely thrived by developing a business structure based on entrepreneurial, family-owned firms that operate easily with one another across national borders. Their business methods are aimed at establishing *trust* as well as lowering transaction costs. This is why most only do business with one another and often with those who speak the same dialect or hale from the same clan. Ethnic Chinese firms as a whole are the biggest foreign investors in China, investing more than the United States, the European Union and Japan combined, mainly moving into the booming south-east coastal provinces, from where most originate.

As the focus of foreign investment shifts further north to Shanghai and Beijing, the importance of clan and language will lose force, according to a study of the overseas Chinese by Australia's Department of Foreign Affairs and Trade. Time, no doubt for the Chinese Diaspora to adapt again, another competitive edge of the overseas Chinese being adaptability, an important characteristic of networking.

Surfers on the Internet can now tap into one of the world's oldest and powerful networking sites, aptly named the 'World Chinese Business Network', the brainchild of Lee Kuan Yew of Singapore.

Control of bamboo networking is passing to a new generation, but as

Asian governments liberalize trade and free their domestic economies, new networking will have to spring up as old *Guanxi* ties loosen, such as alumni of their US business schools, which many of them have attended.

Children are now being groomed for the job more professionally. Typically after an MBA in a Western business school they start work in their early twenties as executives in a division of the family firm. Family businesses all over the world are prone to squabbles; but the proportion of family-controlled firms is exceptionally high in Asia, so the point where the family ends and business begins is seamless.

The principal cause of disputes is usually the line of descent. Sometimes, lacking a male heir, a tycoon will adopt one. Before his death, Sir Y. K. Pao, a Hong Kong shipping and property magnate, divided his empire among his four sons-in-law. Henry Sy, a Chinese emigrant to the Philippines, who now owns half the country's shopping malls, has given his daughter, rather than one of the sons, the lead in running that family business. Increasingly, women are taking on more responsible positions, playing leading roles in the evolving bamboo network. Increasingly the children become networkers in their own right, setting up their own business trading throughout Asia and back into China.

Bangkok Bank was founded by an ethnic Chinese rice-trader, Chin Sophonpanich, who lent only to people he knew, usually on trust or in

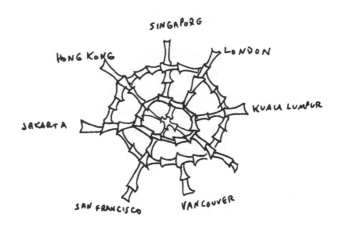

BAMBOO NETWORK — KEY TO SUCCESS
OF 50 MILLION OVERSEAS CHINESE

return for a favour. His Western-educated son, Chatri, has modernized the bank and attracted customers from well outside his father's circle.

Despite exceptions, most families never willingly sell their majority holdings or put their trust in professional managers. As the bamboo network enters cyberspace, it will not be weaker – just different.

Remember the phrase 'The Japanese are coming'? Now the Chinese are coming. But China's potential is not simply a matter of size: the key is the sophisticated, invisible bamboo network, decentralized, Pan-Asian, increasingly global and family/education-orientated, not to mention rich. Chinese around the world hold between two and three trillion dollars in assets. In 1994 the Chinese-language version of *Forbes* magazine analyzed the top 1,000 companies from ten Asian stock markets, adding up to 89 per cent of total market capitalization. Of the top 1000, 517 had an ethnic Chinese as the largest shareholder, controlling 42 per cent of the total. Of the listed companies in a six Asian countries survey by Fujitsu Research in Tokyo, between 50 and 80 per cent were owned by overseas Chinese, making it the third largest economic bloc after the US and Japan. The global economy is dominated by inter-company trade and person-to-person communication, both driven by networks.

When a crisis arises or a great opportunity presents itself, they close ranks and co-operate. If being considered for a new partnership, a personal reference from a respected member of the Chinese business community is worth quite literally its weight in gold. Just as the Internet is a network of about 25,000 networks, the overseas Chinese networks woven together, number in the tens of thousands.

The key to this network is information and influence driven by the market and underpinned by cultural influences. Above all, unlike the Japanese, the Chinese function efficiently as individuals and their autonomous enterprises adapt quickly. Each of the parts functions as if it were the centre of the network. 'There is no prospect working for others', according to the Chinese proverb. Naisbitt believes that the Chinese network is the organizational model for the twenty-first century. 'The world is moving from a collection of nation states to a collection of networks,' he states. It's not who will become part of China that's the question, but who will join the Chinese network.

Today there are an estimated six thousand clan networks in south-east Asia, serving as contact points for employment, news and exchange as well as providing psychological support.

Japanese remain Japanese wherever they journey, the Chinese adopt local habits, language and even names, while not forgetting their roots, investing not only in their adopted homelands but back into mainland China. As children they learned about moral values – mainly Confucian. Terms such as 'business integrity', 'honour', 'your word is your bond' left little scratches on their minds as they ventured forth. Above all they learned the 'morality of the mouth', never to speak ill of others, a value that could be learned in the West.

Lee Kuan Yew saw early on how tiny Singapore could extend its reach, thanks to its airlinks and telecommunications infrastructure, into the most powerful network of all, the overseas Chinese. India could become the next network, numbering about ten million, with an income equivalent to India's GDP. They have been highly successful in the UK, the US, South Africa and Asia.

The other aspect of the network is that created by sending their children to Eton and Harvard, Stanford and Oxford, thus mixing with the West's business and potential elites.

Before Westerners appreciated the value of offshore havens, the overseas Chinese were already there. For now the Chinese are developing Vancouver (where 20 per cent of the population is Chinese) as the operating base for the Dragon Century. As Asian-Americans, the overseas Chinese are reshaping the landscape, especially California, and for the West to plug in to China will require access to it via this truly global tribal network.

John Swire & Sons, one of the wealthiest British family dynasties in Hong Kong, in May 1996 proved the value of the old friends' network by securing a deal to sell further stakes in airlines to the mainland Chinese Citic Pacific, vital to its continuing success in the region, all through a business friendship dating back to the 1940s with Rong Yiren, now Vice-President of China! With the Japanese bubble burst, bureaucrats and politicians are resorting to Japanese values such as collectivism and obedience, rather than taking bold action. Remember the old joke about Pearl Harbour: 'It need never have happened, the Japanese own Hawaii'? Not any more, because they lost more than half the domestic value of the overseas capital invested in the past decade.

Japan is losing market share to the ten emerging Asian tigers, led by China. Because much of its trade is intercorporate, unless Japan welcomes direct foreign investment, little hope exists for correcting its trade imbalance with the rest of the world, a question of culture and networking.

Seppuku, the ritual disembowlment by Japan's feudal warriors to preserve their honour, may be a thing of the past. But an increasing number of the country's corporate samurai are being driven to suicide by the push for restructuring among companies and the flood of scandals resulting from the bureaucratic sclerosis and failure of the economic structure to adapt. Keizan, the network of companies the West find so hard to penetrate, are not going to save Japan in competition with the more open network of connections and degrees of internationalism of the overseas Chinese.

This inability to deal with the changing environment causes stress for office workers who devote their whole lives to the company. Counsellors are telling them to totally change their values and rebuild their lives outside their company via networking! 'Salary men have to realize that their own dreams and those of the company are no longer the same,' says Makato Natsuime, an Osaka psychiatrist.

Some younger Japanese have managed to side-step the cubby-holes and channels that have clogged up the arteries of corporate Japan, by keeping in touch with their 'class of 74' throughout their employment, talking about the real situation as opposed to the official party line. Internal networking may yet rescue Japan from its lack of political will.

In China, as well as in Chinese-dominated businesses throughout Asia, company suitors should give 'face' (honest respect) to a potential partner's decision-makers by investing the personal time of their own leaders. In Asia, partners are selected more for their potential to open doors than for immediate benefits. Lippo Group, a financial conglomerate, has tapped a network of Japanese, European and US partners to expand from its Indonesian home base to China. Founder and Chairman Mochtar Riady believes that promising relationships should be nurtured for their future value, even when initial joint ventures are not very profitable.

Apart from the structural upheaval in Asia, the empowerment of the individual through information and technology has been a major force: 'Information offers choice; choice motivates interaction; and people's interactions form the network of society', according to Jimmy Lai, founder of *Next,* a pro-democracy, pro-market Hong Kong magazine.

Asians, particularly the Chinese, are overlaying onto their traditional value systems new options resulting from their travel and business. The fundamental difference between Western concepts of society and East Asian is that the latter believes the individual exists in the context of family. But the common threads developing between East and West across the Pacific are far more significant than the different values each holds dear. Although no such thing exists as Asian values *per se*, there is no doubt that in the West the rights of the individual have been at the expense of an orderly society, especially in some urban environments, chiefly but not exclusively in the US. A sense of community, which is at the heart of the notion of stakeholder society, is a reflection of the wish to find a moral underpinning to a variety of relationships seen more often in Asia than the West.

The breakdown of trust in our institutions and polity is partly a result of insecurity, partly shortfall of expectations. Francis Fukuyama believes that high levels of trust found in East Asian society help explain the relative stability and success. 'They put trust at the centre of a web of relationships', he writes in his seminal book *Trust: the Social Virtues and the Creation of Prosperity*. The idea is that trust is vital to building long-term relationships between companies and their customers, employees and employers, producers and suppliers. Trust is the most vital component in promoting co-operation as well as competition and is the thinking behind the 'Tomorrow's Company' project discussed elsewhere in the book. High-trust societies foster encouragement and moral pressure in addition to material incentives. Even in low-trust societies in Europe, as Robert Putnam reflects, some Italian regions are very successful because of community encouragement and shared values via networks.

According to a 1995 Gallup survey, 68 per cent of those Chinese questioned said their philosophy was to work hard and get rich, although some referred to giving something back to society. Confucius said, 'If you have wine, you must offer some to your parents and teachers.' With the pace of development and modernization of Asia, many Asians believe a moral grounding is needed, particularly among the young where 'maximization' is in vogue.

Many Asians who went to the US to study and stayed to work in US companies are now seeking wider horizons; they are seen by American management as good work-horses but not race-horses. Well educated and travelled but passed over, they found companies with financial backing from investors in Asia.

Long aware of the value of networking and the informal information chain, they formed their own groups to replace what they lost by stepping outside the establishment. The Asian-American Manufacturers Association, the Chinese Institute of Engineers and the Chinese Software Professionals Association keep executives in Asian-owned companies in the know.

Heidrick and Struggles, the headhunting firm, surveyed 4,000 CEOs in 1993 asking what they looked for in an executive or manager. Almost all said a background in the Asia Pacific, more than two languages, at least one advanced degree and a degree from two countries. Meaning more networking and a new attitude to career management.

Singapore's *Business Times* reports that 'In only one generation some Asian countries have created a crop of career women who are upwardly mobile, globally minded, affluent and ambitious.' That is no mean feat, reflecting another trend.

The paradox is that the more universal we all become economically the more tribal we act in terms of language and cultural identity. But in Asia, families don't work as if they are a joint stock company with no ties of love and duty that bind.

6 Leveraging Lunch: Small-Company Model

'Word of mouth is probably the most powerful
form of communication in the business world.'
Regis McKenna, *The Regis Touch*

'It's not a haphazard approach when you work out
who to speak to, why and what about. Contacts does
not quite explain the notion of networking thoroughly
enough. Networking is more specific, more focused.
Networking makes the (business) world go round.'
Jane Calvert-Lee,
Director, Confederation of British Industry

For a number of years I have been fortunate to be an outside or non-executive director of a small but growing British-based company called Matrix (communications consultants) which achieves scale not by size but by dint of leveraging a 'matrix' of individual and corporate networks.

Specializing in advising companies and governments on complex regulatory and political affairs, especially in emerging markets, Matrix has a variety of individual and corporate shareholdings as well as joint ventures, for example in financial public relations, lobbying, European and international corporate affairs in London as well as in India, Central and Eastern Europe and South Africa, Brussels and Washington. Yet it remains a small core team at the centre but with access to infrastructure, expertise and arms-and-legs support in key sectors and countries. It's not a virtual company in the sense of one I know which has a whole host of networking notables on its advisory board and use of part-time consultants, but at the centre is quite literally co-ordinated by one man and his dog. Matrix is nevertheless at the virtual end of the spectrum not wishing to become a large group by virtue of excessive organic or acquisition growth as discussed in Chapter 7. Yet the principle of partnerships leveraging the network remains the same.

Having run a small business and invested in another (which I have been proud to see grow rapidly), not to mention having advised small companies, I have learnt some very important rules about networking, which so many don't take seriously either because they can't see the wood for the trees or don't believe in it.

McKinsey & Co., the management consultancy, is the 'ultimate project organization'. 'Create your own firm' is one of the company's maxims, constantly redeveloping itself in a flexible, adaptable way, building networks being a key activity. Of course, McKinsey is not small relatively speaking, but like all consultancies, the output is produced by small project teams with a combination of inside and outside experts always working close to the customer.

The organizing principles of McKinsey are increasingly the role model for small, service businesses, particularly consultancies:

1 Knowledge work is now the main source of value-added.
2 Seamless horizontal networks with no middle management.
3 Project teams focusing on promoting interdependence between team members via trust and nurturing talent.
4 Outsiders 'belong' to the company, a key element of the network.
5 Organizational learning, including maximum access to information is an essential prerequisite.
6 Power in the marketplace resides in the significance of networks rather than the resources of the organization.
7 Everything is global but 'new big' means 'network big'.
8 There exists a culture of databases and library fora for discussion of ideas and sharing information (McKinsey even has a Director of Knowledge Management).
9 'Systems Integrators' establish and manage networks.
10 It contains some paradoxes – autonomy of individuals working in partnership within a certain amount of organized disorganization and, most important, 'networking big' while remaining physically small.

This brings us onto 'relationship marketing' without which no book on networking would be complete. Even though it is not synonymous with networking, the two are inter-related when discussing the way small 'enterprise webs' should function, particularly when related to their own marketing.

Theodore Levitt in his book *The Marketing Imagination* defined the purpose of business as being to create and keep a customer. So far so good. He believes the emphasis is moving from a transaction to a relationship focus, touched on elsewhere in this book, thanks to an increasing number of stakeholders, not least the internal market and a shift from an emphasis on a single sale to customer retention, concentrating on benefits not features, long term not short term.

The challenge therefore of relationship marketing is to bring the three circles of service, quality and marketing more closely into alignment around not just customers, vital as they are, but employees and recruits, suppliers, referrers and influencers such as third-party endorsers and those who will help achieve the output, i.e. those the company can learn from or to which the client or customer needs access. The successful company in this mode does not concentrate only on structure, strategy and systems but shared values, skills training, staff motivation and shared values (McKinsey's '7s' methodology).

Ultimately people should be at the centre of marketing, which is not just about price, process, place, product and promotion but about people. The strong ties that bind, a key theme of this book are, says Levitt 'solid competitive barriers'. Some of course believe that social ties confound business relationships but this is based on an erroneous assumption that business decisions are made in an interpersonal vacuum.

As Keith Blois of Templeton College, Oxford University Management School, points out, various definitions of 'relationship marketing' are couched in terms of desired outputs and do not indicate the required inputs to determine if a relationship marketing policy is being successfully pursued. However most studies agree that activities which create commitment and trust take time as well as being expensive, but with the intent of establishing a long-term relationship.

The objective of relationship marketing is to turn new customers into social advocates for the company, thus playing an important role as a referral source. The successful relationship marketeer convinces clients or customers that he or she has their interests at heart while at the same time pursuing the company's own agenda.

Reich uses the apt phrase 'enterprise web' when describing the often global network of individuals and small companies with a skill at brokering solutions, 'strategic brokers' at the centre of a multi-talent network, netweaving, i.e. managing a variety of overlapping networks pulling together the nodes and the links. To solve problems in our complex, diverse, interdependent world at least ten new networks need to be created by a new and growing small business. If you are wanting to build a business in India and you are based in London, it's vital to tap not just those organizations in the UK trading with India but connect with the Indian community based in London. But it is interesting that while networking is not free, people don't want to pay for it! Facilitators and catalysts will eventually be able to package a product but this gift is rarely perceived as value-added. Public relations and related disciplines come closest to it.

Networking is often overlooked as a mainstream communication technique, yet it is often a highly influential form of communications. I believe it to be an essential ingredient. As these networks often operate informally they tend not to be regarded as part of an organization's formal channel of communication. The growing importance of networking and the reasons for it have been described earlier in this book, but can be partially attributed to increasing societal fragmentation, tending to make mass-media channels relatively ineffective at reaching, let alone influencing highly specialized target publics. Organizations have recognized the importance of 'tapping' into the various informal networks that exist within different sections of society. It's the difference between 'broadcasting' and 'narrowcasting' in a media sense and between the 'machine gun' and 'rifle' approach in a marketing sense. Networking has always been more serendipity than enlightened, more luck than judgement. What has changed is the formal recognition of networking as part of an organization's communication strategy. Although many networks may form quite naturally out of the common interests which different groups of people and company partnerships possess, a systematic approach requires the deliberate creation of networks with the aim of engineering a potentially influential channel of communication. Most people belong to networks without being conscious of them. If you're running a company, networks, if properly formed and managed, are a valuable resource. Ironically the more virtual the company, being the spider in the web requires even more management!

For the small company therefore, particularly a consultancy where networking is the lifeblood, company leadership must identify networks that can be tapped for the benefit of the customer or client as well as to obtain the right information on people to assist. But above all it exists to assist the company with its own marketing. If it is accepted that the best customers or clients derive from referrals, it doesn't happen just by serendipity. Of course if you do a good job, the odd client will recommend you and if your work is in the public arena the output will speak for itself. But how many small businesses have access to that?

If it is also accepted that the key to effective networking is an alignment of relevant information, issues and interface, then the point of departure for a small-company marketing programme is to define these issues on which you can give appropriate 'thought-leadership', research those 'opinion-formers' who would be useful and appropriate people to have a dialogue with on those issues by virtue of their knowledge and interest to your customers or prospects, directly and indirectly, and which interfaces you need to attract into your web via networking.

A rule-of-thumb is that an organization is more likely to get its message across and acted upon if it uses a mix (obviously appropriate) of techniques. So naturally if you can afford it and it hits the right audience, advertising may be as appropriate as mailing your brochure to a bunch of prospects. But all this should be properly databased and those you really want to interface with hit three to five times a year. This can be done by Christmas card, mailing the annual review, the occasional bi-lateral lunch, a speaking engagement, so long as it is all part of a coherent programme of activity. But above all, there's no substitute for an 'issues (or focus) lunch', for which the guests are properly researched.

Sandra Macleod, the Chief Executive of Carma International, a media content analysis firm she has built up in Europe as part of a global group founded by my friend Al Barr in the US, runs these all the time as an integral part of the marketing programme which embraces all the above techniques. The company works at it systematically and it has paid off. But these lunches require a terrific networking approach because not only the issue for discussion over lunch but the guest list is chosen with precision. So that clients are interspersed with prospects, key opinion-formers whom clients and prospects want to meet attend as well as journalists and academics (together with opinion-formers) who may write an editorial or undertake some research respectively.

Carole Stone (an ex-BBC Producer of 'Any Questions'), and one of London's truly great networkers, says she does it without thinking. She organizes lunches for friends as well as for companies and carefully mixes and matches. The secret, she believes, is to make people feel as if they are not coming to lunches and meeting you as a favour but because they know it will be constructive and enjoyable as part of an informal but structured network.

According to another great London networker, Jean Wadlow, who organizes similar lunches on a personal and corporate basis, it's a question of systematic contact marketing, storing of contact in the memory for when they're needed and tight or broad targeting, depending on the issue, interface and information nature of the lunch (or other event). Above all she believes 'Life does a complete cycle' so it is important to think of networking long term, therefore ensuring the research is about the people one needs to meet, that one is in the right networks and above all that one provides exactly the appropriate forum within which to network.

It is significant that both Carole Stone and Jean Wadlow state categorically that they don't network consciously, they just do it; I think from observing them that they protest too much!

John Smythe, of Smythe Dorward Lambert, a company which has established a solid niche in the field of 'change management', is someone I have admired for his systematic approach to relationship marketing and networking. Just like Sandra Macleod, he works hard at ensuring that he not only mixes in the right networks of relevance to his own marketing and client needs but invites targets to regular functions and, in between times, mail-shots them not just newsletters but relevant 'thought pieces'. He's even set up his company's very own network, a series of courses on subjects appropriate to his sphere of influence, thus reinforcing the company's credibility as well as advancing the state of knowledge. How's that for a captive audience?

The Confederation of British Industry formally networks as it realizes the importance of cross-fertilization of ideas and it is of benefit because it enables people to lift their eyes from the immediate task. But it also networks on behalf of its members. Jane Calvert-Lee, Director of the Confederation of British Industry in London explains that they hold weekly lunches on a variety of subjects which will enable people from one sector to share experiences with those from another. To ensure she has a good crop of people to invite she always prepares herself when invited to other networks by undertaking research into who she should be talking to and on what subjects (information, issues and interfaces) she should put into her networking memory bank.

As barriers break down and interdependence grows, networking will play an even larger role. People and companies cannot afford to close their eyes to anything. In the past manufacturing industry would just be looking to meet people in their particular industry: that is no longer sufficient, if still necessary.

Now insurance companies can learn from car companies: they both process data. In Japan the motor industry teaches other industries about data processing. Countries, languages, sectors, functions are being broken down such that one area of information and knowledge spills over into another, making networking all the more important, if all the more difficult. Small companies therefore can't just wait for the knock on the door for the odd referral which never comes, or meet the few contacts they know, to become successful. If they really want to be at the centre of the enterprise web, undertake interesting assignments and earn some money into the bargain, then they must invest time and money into a sustained and systematic networking/relationship marketing programme. None of this can be done without hard effort, identifying the right networks, and a great deal of research, identifying who you as a company want on your database and how often and with what means to reach them.

Many small-business leaders live in a management cocoon, living inside the company rather than maintaining a balance, dealing chiefly with customers externally and forgetting about broader stakeholders and networkers. The Young President's Organization (where members have to be a CEO before age 40 and leave at 50) is a good network for example, as are the university alumni. The Junior Chamber of Commerce is another good network in the UK. There are similar in Brussels such as the American Chamber of Commerce and the Junior Women's League in Washington DC.

In putting together a lunch recognize the difference between an opinion-former as leaders or followers. Opinion-formers network with change agents to get the news, and adopters to relay it. This affects whom you invite. Be careful to follow up after the lunch and keep in touch five times a year. Eighty per cent of sales are made over the fifth call! Belong to a good networking club, not just for sales leads but intelligence gathering and relationship-building. It could also be fun, an essential ingredient of the networking philosophy. Having fun is never easy in a business and professional sense, but if it isn't fun, it isn't worth the candle.

Networking is integrative, it's inside-out. As with individuals, small companies need to understand the difference between the inner circle, the friend network, the business network, how you handle them and how often you interface. Ask yourself as head of this small and hopefully growing business, does any net work for me and my organization? Does it fit with my one-year and five-year plan, are there any network gaps and how do I fill them?

Ultimately it is about strategy not tactics, a mind-set, a technique a company should use consistently to build links with people and partnerships to share anything mutually beneficial.

As in personal networking it all exists for advice, information, support, energy and above all referrals, which are worth their weight in gold. It requires a focusing of energy. It's not a game, but using resources around you to gather and distribute information, ideas and contacts.

I suppose some are born to connections, others have to work at it. The latter applies to most of us.

7 The Art of Alliances: a Corporate Model

'Like romances, alliances are built on hopes and dreams – what might happen if certain opportunities are pursued.'

Rosabeth Moss Kanter

'For organizations to get in shape for Olympic competition they must evolve flatter, more focused organizations, stressing synergies . . . extending reach without increasing size.'

Rosabeth Moss Kanter

Today we see groups of companies linking together for a common purpose, in the automotive field, in biotechnology, in three converging industries: telecommunications, computers, and media resulting from digitalization. These alliances give companies access to skills in different countries, complementary technologies, investment sharing and the like. Networks spring up because competition becomes less worthwhile than co-operation – co-opetition as it's called.

The new BskyB, Bertelsmann and Canal Plus Alliance planning more than one hundred channels of digital satellite TV in Germany, moving into Italy, is a case in point. If you can't beat them join them!

Ronald Allen, CEO of Delta Airlines in Atlanta, acknowledges that collaborative alliances are a modern-day fact of life, the most useful being those in which each partner strives to obtain a competitive advantage for the other: the relationships get even better if they also build value for the customers.

Building trust within relationships asks for two basic qualities, according to Allen. The relationship must be needed by both sides with long-term goals clearly dependent on its success. It must also be founded on genuine, honest communications, with detailed business information as well as management concepts shared freely.

The Delta CEO explains that during re-engineering of its huge maintenance division, a decision was made to share goals with suppliers. This

ALLIANCES ARE LIKE
ROMANCES

resulted in one supplier coming forward with a plan that saved all the jobs in one of the shops. In exchange for a long-term contract, costs and prices were lowered. The value most likely to be gained from these ventures is mutual trust. In a volatile world market, trust that derives from open exchange and clear communication can provide a huge competitive advantage.

Business alliances must yield benefits for partners beyond just the deal, involving collaboration, not just exchange, added value rather than mere barter. Keith Blois, Fellow in Marketing at Templeton College, Oxford, sums it up thus: 'Relationships grow organically over time cumulatively adding to their stock of benefits', although he was referring to the informal relationships between college and companies undertaking management development programmes. The principle however is the same. These relationships, alliances and partnerships are not controllable by formal systems but require a dense web of interpersonal connections which enhance learning.

In the US, where businesses generally adopt a narrow adversarial view of a relationship (hence the success of the legal profession), preoccupied with the economics of the deal, they often neglect the political, cult, organizational and human aspects of a partnership. Continental Europe is somewhere in the middle of the spectrum of sensitivity to the soft arts, with Asia best (see Chapter 5). The keys to success here are individual empowerment, a culture of interdependence, sharing information and investment. In the uncertain, fast-changing global company, companies are known by the company they keep! Inter-company relations are a key business asset and knowing how to nurture the network an essential management skill.

As Moss Kanter quite rightly asserts, 'Business alliances are living systems, evolving progressively in their possibilities.' In a research project involving thirty-seven companies and their partners from eleven parts of the world, Moss Kanter uncovered three fundamental aspects. First, beyond the immediate reasons for entering into a relationship, making the connection offers the parties an option in the future, opening new doors to unforeseen opportunities. Second, relations that both parties ultimately deem successful create new value and synergies. Third, they cannot be controlled but require internal infrastructures that enhance trust and learning.

In summary, successful alliances succeed by first acquiring knowledge and then effectively managing the human aspects of their alliances. What's more there's always the potential for additional collaboration. The strongest are 'value-chain' partnerships such as supplier–customer relationships referred to earlier. Companies in different industries with different but complementary skills link their capabilities to create value for ultimate users. But the relationships can be many and varied with partners wearing several hats – gatekeeper, investor, owner, supplier, customer etc.

The characteristics of effective inter-company relationships challenge many decades of Western economic and managerial assumptions. Although smaller companies, family businesses and those operating in 'developing' countries have largely retained 'pre-modern' characteristics, the rational model has been considered the ideal to which all organizations would eventually conform.

Inter-company relationships are different. They seem to work best when more family-like and less rational, where obligations are more diffuse, understanding grows between specific individuals, communication is frequent and intensive and the inter-personal context is rich. The key to success is individual excellence by both parties – adding value, being positive and showing integrity. When information is not abused, the relationship is win/win.

You will have gathered that relationships between companies begin, grow and develop – and fail – in ways similar to relationships between people: the eight 'I's that create successful 'We's' of individual excellence, importance, interdependence, investment, information, integration, institutionalization and integrity, to summarize Moss Kanter's research.

Foote, Cone and Belding, and Publicis, the two advertising agencies, only later found a remarkable degree of similarity in their creative operating philosophies. At the outset, although from different vantage points, both had the same imperative – to expand their international reach, and the same catalyst: their mutual client Nestlé was reducing its agencies from 100 to five. But the FCB–Publicis alliance is evidence that, especially in fast-moving industries, potential partners must find compatibility in legacy, philosophy and desires, because specific opportunities are often short-lived and won't sustain a long-term relationship.

The best agreements between companies contain several important components: first, a specific joint activity to make the relationship real; second, side-bets such as equity swap, or exchange of personnel reflecting a willingness to connect the fates of the companies; and third, clear signals of continuing independence for all partners, like appointing an American to the European joint-venture.

Active collaborations take place when companies develop mechanisms – structures, processes and skills – for bridging organizational and inter-personal differences. Multiple ties at multiple levels ensure communication, co-ordination and control; more, rather than fewer people need to be devoted to relationship activities.

According to Moss Kanter, the most productive relationships achieve five levels of *integration – strategic,* involving continuing contact among the leadership; *cultural,* requiring people to have the requisite communications skills to bridge the differences; *inter-personal,* where the network of personal ties grows in extent and density (formal structures don't work unless the relationship exists); *operational* whereby ways are found to participate in training programmes, share people, information etc.; and *tactical,* which brings middle-level professionals together in teamnets to develop projects.

Productive relationships usually require and often stimulate changes within the partners. This means that relationship managers must be empowered to vary their own company's procedures. This also provides an infrastructure for learning. Companies with strong communications across functions and widely shared information tend to have more productive external relationships.

Many businesses fail to realize the full potential from their partnerships because internal barriers to communication limit learning to the small cadre of people directly involved in the relationship. Alliances benefit from establishing multiple, independent centres of competence and innovation. Each centre can pursue different paths, creating in turn new networks that go off in new directions. Flexibility and openness are critical attitudes in forming and even ending alliances, where integrity remains crucial. If not, future relationships will be jeopardized, especially in Asian countries, where everyone has long memories!

Entente – the striking of an alliance – is a responsible part of a strategist's repertoire, particularly in a changeable world of rapidly globalizing markets and industries. Keniche Ohmae of McKinsey's Tokyo office believes that while globalization mandates alliances, making them absolutely essential to strategy, managers and corporations are wary of them, because alliances mean sharing control, contacts and competitor information. Of course it's a risk, a commitment has to be made and it could turn out to be a Trojan Horse. There is also the impression that alliances represent at best a convenience, betraying as in personal networking a short-term, quick in-and-out attitude. Unless the long-term strategy value of entente is understood, frustration will set in when it proves not to be cheap or easy.

Alliances should not be viewed, according to Ohmae, as 'tools of convenience'. They are 'important, even critical, instruments of serving customers in a global environment'. Glaxo, the British pharmaceutical company, did not want to establish a full business system in each country where it did business. Especially given its costly commitment to top-flight R&D, it did not want to build an extensive sales and service network to cover all the hospitals in Japan and the US. So it linked up with first-class partners in Japan, swapped its best drugs with them and focused its own resources on generating greater sales from its established network in Europe. Few companies operating in Japan, Europe and the US can offer such top-flight levels of values to all their customers all the time all by themselves. 'They need partners. They need entente. They might wish things were otherwise. But deep down they know better or they should,' says Ohmae, more in hope than expectation. Many global or regional PR networks (not all) fail because they don't adhere to these principles. The more successful affiliation networks emphasize they are not a paper network. They operate as a separate corporation and compete with the large multi-national firms. They provide geographic representation and marketing clout via shared resources and intelligence. But once personal involvement is lost through size, the glue that holds the network together is lost. Inconsistency or the weak link can just as easily be levelled at wholly owned global PR firms as networks, so you take your pick. There are arguments for both.

It's clear from these analyses that in the changing world described earlier, alliances are corporate networks requiring the same approaches and attitudes as personal networking. As with personal networking, corporate alliances are increasingly important forms of relationship based on *trust, long-term thinking* and *mutuality.*

ICL, the Japanese-owned computer company based in the UK, in its 'Do's for successful collaboration' emphasizes mutual respect and mutual expectations, trust and personal commitment. In today's uncertain world with dangerous opponents, going alone is not an option.

Baker Jardine, which has used technological expertise to forge a niche in an area dominated by oil giants, has a competitive edge: it stands at the gateway to the M4 motorway (just outside London) innovation network, the high-tech corridor that stretches west from London along the motorway to Bristol, centring on Swindon. The aim of the network is to enable small companies to learn about the use of modern technology, both from each other and from larger companies that have joined the network such as 3M and National Power. Those behind the network (a crucial alliance between government, technology centres, small and large businesses), believe that bringing together the expertise of universities, training and enterprise centres and larger companies is a key way for small companies to prosper. Although not a member of the innovation network, Baker Jardine holds an impressive record of links with oil companies such as BP and Conoco. But for its next phase of expansion the company will need the kind of connections the network provides. John Howell, Chairman of the M4 innovation network (with potentially 7,000 members) and UK technology manager at 3M argued that the rationale was to improve business knowledge and technical transfer. Howell cites one small company that started up and six months later was marketing a medical product globally!

In future small and larger companies will need to work more closely together to keep the sharks at bay, says Howell: 'To survive, small companies have to be both innovative and look at collaboration.'

An alliance by British Energy with USA-based Westinghouse and Teneo, the Spanish industrial group in early 1996 brings together complementary skills and capabilities in building/operating nuclear power stations. According to a company statement, this agreement by a company that previously relied solely on its UK domestic electricity-generating market, 'allows us to market our combined expertise internationally'.

With no one company or country having a monopoly of experience, skills and technology across the full range of nuclear reactor services and a vast potential market in Asia, an alliance of this kind is quite natural, especially as in this field there has always been close collaboration between companies and across the industry globally, sharing technical and safety knowledge.

Collaboration in business is no longer confined to conventional two-company alliances. Today groups of companies are linking themselves together for a common purpose leading to a new form of co-operation – group versus group. The individual companies may differ in size and focus, but they fulfil specific roles within the group. Furthermore, within the network, companies may be linked to one another through various kinds of alliances, ranging from the formality of an equity joint venture to the informality of a loose collaboration.

Primarily there is a need to gain scale economies as market-share, and who joins depends on patterns of growth. These clusters or constellations, pioneered in the computer field, join together in an overlapping relationship with collective governance ensuring that a network is more than a haphazard collection of alliances.

Francis Bidault and Thomas Cummings of IMD Management School, Switzerland, writing in the *Financial Times*, believe that senior executives are becoming increasingly aware of a range of hidden benefits from alliances. Hidden benefits come in the form of innovations derived from detailed presentations of each side's expertise, the potential for improvement exposed in applying existing expertise to a new situation, and the pressure to perform from a demanding partner. Ultimately a common benefit of all alliances is that they expose more of an organization to the real world out there. Manufacturing and R&D for example are often only indirectly exposed to what is happening in the market. Alliance partners can introduce new threats as well as new opportunities. Alliances are a good weapon to combat one of the most common diseases afflicting successful companies, namely complacency.

Just over two per cent of UK manufacturing companies were world class in 1994, according to a study by IBM and London Business School (14/41 in the World Economic Forum ranking). This results, as you might expect, from complacency, concentration on narrow financial performance, which doesn't adequately measure the health of the company, product quality, speed of response and service, and not least, the national adversarial heritage. This makes partnerships with suppliers and customers difficult.

The 'Tomorrow's Company' project sponsored by a variety of companies and led by the Royal Society of Arts sees 'Relationships as the underlying source of competitiveness', not just relationships with shareholders, but an 'inclusive' approach involving all stakeholders. The Chairman is Sir Anthony Cleaver, formally of IBM UK, now Chairman of AEA Technology. He says that in 1994, 80 per cent of managers would serve investors before other stakeholders (including alliances and partners). Now only 60 per cent would adopt that position.

Sir Colin Marshall, Chairman of British Airways, believes that business plans should be shared with suppliers, so that a long-term view can be taken together. Allan Willett, Chairman of Willett International, the product coding company, stresses collaboration with the competition. Lloyds Register, the UK shipping federation, collaborates with US and Norwegian competition to devise new safety-at-sea activities.

The Unipart group of companies, under the inspirational John Neill, set up a partnership with its dealers, driven by the realization that it was in their mutual interest. It's called the 'shared destiny' relationship. This was the first such relationship with key stakeholders short of a formal alliance, but a partnership nevertheless. 'The inclusive model is not based on altruism or a soggy collectivism. It is very demanding, based on trust, something which is very difficult for Westerners to grasp,' says Neill.

Hopefully with the world getting smaller, without imposing one form of capitalism on another, values can be shared that help companies, governments, NGOs and other groups to work together in 'partnership'.

The issues are global, more complex, requiring consensus on a long-term basis. With the systematic decline in political leadership and the growth in power of the pressure groups, which often operate on a global basis via networking, working together for a single purpose, corporations, via stakeholding, need to develop positions on key issues such as education and training, unemployment (both of graduates and the over-55s) and the environment. This is particularly so with companies moving into the transition economies of Central and Eastern Europe which require partnerships and alliances not only with local companies and host governments but local authorities, NGOs, funding agencies, universities and other groups, all of which require new skills not needed in the past, more dialogue, and less adversarialism.

With the trend towards privatization and deregulation in this part of the world (as elsewhere), the three prongs of sustainable development are not just economics or even environmental protection but also 'social equity'. Increasingly it will be private capital that has to pave the way via leadership, dialogue, partnerships, often informal, networking. In Hungary and the Czech Republic one of the stakeholders is the citizen, whether a shareholder or customer of the business or not.

The planet is not some sub-set of the global economy but of the biosphere, yet governments (it's better at local level) lack a 'brokerage' role at central level. If business therefore doesn't rise to the occasion, then the formal politician process won't be able to ensure social stability and stable consumer markets. It's often said we live in a hard age needing hard facts, that all of the above is just soft values. Following the 'Brent Spar' oil platform episode Shell recognized that co-operation and dialogue must replace managing issues and 'We-know-best' communications. In an interdependent world, corporations and other institutions must work together to find solutions not just in a narrow, vested-interest way but adopting a holistic approach based on trusting relationship building. So values have become *hard*. Global consumers have become world citizens. Materialism has become holism, responsibilities have replaced rights and people are thinking long- rather than short-term.

If one takes the much abused term 'sustainability', which is the spur to much of the thinking and ask people what it means, words like 'open', 'principled', 'evolving' and 'searching' spring to mind, according to a company called 'Sustainability', an environmental consultancy. They argue that 'searching' people are 'inter-cultural', 'cross-boundary', 'multifaceted', 'engaged' and 'networked'.

Companies, like individuals, must look beyond their formal alliances to more informal partnerships when dealing with sustainable development. The last decade of the millennium has seen unprecedented business opportunities in new markets, the removal of inefficiencies and new freedoms of movement. On the other hand we have seen the emergence of insecurities, growing gaps between those who profit from reform and those who lose out with its implications for disillusionment with change.

As Prince of Wales Business Leaders Forum CEO Robert Davies says,

'Business can optimize the spin-off from its activities to assist transition through human resources development, assisting supply and distribution chains, improving the environment, working in public/private partnerships and playing an active role in communities.' But it requires a win/win attitude based on trust and an inclusive approach new to most Westerners.

8 The Autonomous Employee: the Internal Market Model

'By binding the new company–employee
relationship in continued mutual seduction and choice
rather than on a resentful acceptance of one-way
dependence, the new contract is not just effective, but moral.'
The World in 96, Groshel LBS/Bartlett HBS

'Top managers generally speak half the time and
don't listen the other half.'   Helmut Maucher, CEO Nestlé

I was headhunted to join Ford Motor Company relatively late in life, entering at VP (the 'Marine Corps' as it is affectionately known). Although I was respected for the skills I brought to the party and had power by dint of office, in retrospect I had one great disadvantage (in addition to being the poor relation in terms of budget). The average length of service being in excess of twenty years, whatever my title, I was severely constrained in getting things done, lacking an internal network. This was confounded by a constant conflict, unique to my function (public affairs and government relations) of needing to network externally (by definition) yet only achieving knowledge and credibility by attending internal meetings, usually long ones!

3M Corporation has a dilemma. It always believed in 'lifelong careers', but because of mergers and closures this has become impossible. The conundrum now is how to motivate staff to be innovative while addressing costs resulting in overwork and insecurity.

The key to both these examples resides in the growing inter-relationship between internal and external networking, both for the company's sake and the employees', particularly given the individual's need to control his or her own career development and the onus on the company to provide an empowered internal environment, involving cross-functional teams and opportunities for informal knowledge-sharing networks. Shell Oil Company recognize a new organizational contract, whereby the company undertakes to improve the 'future employability' of its people.

With the shift away from paternalistic career planning and the changing

TOP MANAGERS
GENERALLY SPEAK
HALF THE TIME AND DON'T LISTEN
THE OTHER HALF

nature of the employer–employee relationship, the autonomous employee requires new skills, networking skills among others, enabling them to build a wide personal infrastructure of contacts, spanning other companies, headhunters, business schools, mentors and national borders. Top managers must be able to challenge the conventional paradigm, to be able to think outside their box. Peter Waine of Hanson-Green, specialists in part-time directorships, believes that aspiring managing directors should go on subsidiary boards of other companies to gain experience. It's obviously important to generate support and energy from mentors as well as colleagues, so they become co-conspirators in owning your career.

Charles Handy's Shamrock Model, with its three leaves of 'core professionals', the 'contractual fringe' and 'part-time workers' is gaining ground, allowing talented people who gain experience, learn and network to flourish. Those individuals who are able to understand both the internal market and the complex web of relationships producing multiple collaborations, some internal, some external, will be highly prized in the new environment.

Research by the UK's Industrial Society shows that about fifty per cent of the country's employers make 'some' use of mentoring. Not everyone has the innate qualities to be the ideal mentor and it is a mistake to believe it is synonymous with 'influence' or 'seniority'. Nor is it about teaching, rather counselling and inter-personal skills. From this respondents find the ability to widen their perspectives, develop their potential faster and increase their motivation. Mentoring works from the top floor to the shop floor and David Clutterbuck, the management author, has set up a business in this field to prove it.

Rosabeth Moss Kanter says that sustaining competitiveness involves '3 C's' – concepts, competence and *contacts!* With more and more internal consultants and even full-time employees having to be persuaded rather than forced, the most effective work is often undertaken via networking rather than through formal channels.

Particularly in computer companies, the environment is ripe for internal networking. As people become more specialist it's vital that the team leader knows the best people for the job in hand. These people then have to be persuaded to undertake that job. Given many overlapping circles of expertise and parallel groups of different configurations, which group is chosen will largely depend on networking.

With each job tailored to the client in companies like IBM and few formal progression channels, people spending a great deal of time away from the office, coffee areas within office complexes assume an important networking role, supported by the E-Mail of course. Naturally people tend to network with those who joined the company at the same time. People work together for a period of time and then once the team breaks up, the project leader knows who to call on next time. But in IBM as in other companies of its ilk, there are few personnel officers and there is personal responsibility for career progression. Because everyone is operating within teams, staff never feel part of a large hierarchy, which nevertheless makes it important to network horizontally into other groups. External networking is also important, with former clients for example.

IBM recently set up a cross-organizational network of people, designed to look at breaking down the inevitable compartments. Any part of IBM anywhere in the world can sign up for a group called 'Management Decision Support', which recently held a meeting in Orlando, Florida for 200 people. For this a database of like-minded people has been created onto

Lotus Notes – an extremely useful networking tool. People feel empowered by being part of such a group. There are twenty or so similar groups within IBM. It enables people to avoid reinventing the wheel by sharing information and building up intellectual capital. Obviously information technology has been an enabler for networking.

At the meeting in Orlando, IBM adopted a conference technique called 'Open Space'. For one-and-a-half days they had no specific agenda but allowed people to suggest discussion groups they would like to run. So they splintered off into many different groups. This idea grew out of a comment that the most useful part of conferences are the coffee breaks!

The best-managed companies network internally, what ABB calls the 'internal market', where colleagues in other departments are either suppliers or customers. Highly divisionalized companies need to network internally, for example to 'share sales leads' and bridge the gaps. Technical expertise as much as marketing information is just as susceptible to networking.

David Clutterbuck breaks down internal networking into two – *information networks*, how to find out what's going on; and *influence* networks, how to get things done. Most managers need both in order to operate. These can be easily mapped, i.e. if there are five key things to do, there are five types of information one needs to have, therefore how many approaches does one need to make to obtain it?

Research undertaken by INSEAD in Fontainbleu, France, surveying the electronics industry found that although employees were expected to use the hierarchy, they actively preferred using their informal networks.

There is much more power to be gained by being the informal purveyor of information, the gateway to resources. (Formal networks are only used for rubber-stamping and resolving conflict, i.e. the informal network has broken down.) The finance director is often more powerful than the COO or MD for this reason, hence the reason why the financial director of a Japanese company in the UK is invariably a Japanese.

Inside a company networkers are looking for advancement opportunities or to get a job done, whereas outside networking is more about adding breadth to experiences, lifetime learning and only sometimes seeking another job.

The autonomous employee needs to understand that networks are portable, they help get the job done, but they also position one for the future. Companies are now encouraging employees to communicate more and connect with professional and personal networks, to practise daily the game plan, know their direction, examine their purpose and parlay them to benefit their social life, community, career but also their company. Networking is an inside job.

Within companies, executives need to develop the ability to assemble teams and secure resources as well as manage external alliances and partnerships with customers, suppliers and even competitors, increasingly in a global context.

Network organizations are replacing traditional hierarchies by knocking down walls, between functions/departments/divisions as well as between customers, suppliers, competitors, investors. In the move from high-volume to high-value enterprises, formal rank/position becomes irrelevant due to the continuous linkage between solutions and needs. Every person in the firm forms (or should form) a nexus of relations. We are not free-floating independent atoms, but a node in a network of relations.

Re-engineering the corporation is about making the connections and building relations about processes, not roles. In the newly structured firms it is the span of co-ordination rather than control requiring technical but also relationship skills. Everyone should develop networking skills; people with them should be hired and rewarded for them and trained if they have that gap.

A new kind of business hero is emerging with inspirations, enabling, empowerment and communication skills replacing control, boss, intimidation skills – soft values for a hard decade! With people, values, culture being so vital to competitiveness and productivity, it is surprising how so many companies (GE's Jack Welch excepted) suffer serious disability when it comes to networking skills, communicating and leadership.

Dr Jon White, a consultant and visiting Professor of Public Affairs at City University Business School in London, believes it is vital to understand the communication structure of a company as well as its culture and formal organization. It is important to develop an image of the network one is dealing with, who is in it, and what role they play in it. Are they communication stars (do they have many contacts within the network) or are they on the periphery of the network?

Women are good networkers within the new style of organization, but often seek external support to recharge their batteries.

Geraldine Sharpe-Newton of Turner Broadcasting (CNN) believes 'networking is about a group of like-minded people who may be in the same place in their careers. It could be looked upon as offering opportunities as well as being helpful in discussing career options.

'I don't believe that men on what is known as the 'old boy network' are actually networking, but when wining and dining each other they are doing exactly what we women are doing.'

CNN, as a news organization, operates with a very open philosophy whereby anyone can talk to anyone and because of its deadline nature everyone learns quickly how to communicate messages. Sharpe-Newton belongs to the International Women's Forum.

Another female TV executive, who has also worked at Number 10 Downing Street, says her life in TV, politics and journalism has had three essential ingredients – contacts, gossip and alcohol! Mentoring a few younger women, she advises that the first person you need to get to know in a new job is the telephone receptionist as well as the PA to the Chairman. Women may be more self-conscious networkers but men are more conscious of status. Because women often don't know the rules of how to move through the system, they should, she advises, build up trust, understand the vulnerabilities of the person they are meeting and always be positive.

Barbara Beck, a journalist with the *Economist* and first Chairwoman of London's Reform Club (who like some others doesn't use the term 'networking', believing it to be a subtle art rather than requiring a systematic approach), says 'Business has always been a question of whom you know. But some senior businessmen are surprisingly not very good at it. Some of them need an intermediary to introduce them to the right people.'

Networking is more than just exchanging information with associates when necessary: it is a complete business development strategy. But everyone agrees that apart from more and improved sources of information and ability to share problems with colleagues you also need to network externally to obtain valuable snippets of information, make contacts and generally keep up-to-date.

There is certainly a lack of systematic analysis or coherent methodology but there exists an 'intuitive notion' at least that networking may become fundamental to organizations; indeed will dictate their shape. There is a balance to be struck between control of an organization and unleashing the human, high-tech, innovative side of business, namely networking. The Luddites will hold back this trend but it will be a struggle between the Orwellian mentality and Renaissance Man (and Woman) – the Polymath mentality as I prefer to call it.

People's values, expectations and exploding information sources such as cyberspace are confounding traditional management paradigms, human networking beyond the computer.

ADL, the consulting firm, believes that limited resources, yet limitless problems, lead inexorably to networking, hence their Christmas networking parties. According to ADL, hierarchy is too inefficient to avoid conflicts, the key to networks being personal respect, trust and charisma.

With fourteen million businesses in the US, only two million of which are corporations, eleven million proprietorships and one million partnerships, the bulk of US business is held together by networks, principally by netweavers who initiate and co-ordinate networks, pulling nodes and links together.

The *Economist* in an editorial states that 'computers and human networks bypass central authority and controls and that's welcome'. Although, as debates in the UK about corporate governance point out, the internal boardroom networks (non-executive or outsider directors) on the largest company boards, friends sitting on each other's boards will result in ever-diminishing returns.

The large corporations have earned for themselves an influential position, exercising political and social muscle as well as generating and distributing most of the wealth. This influence scarcely existed fifty years ago. And in fifty years' time it may have evaporated. Although the 'churning' in the computer world may have made most companies more productive it has tended to erode their legitimacy. In the tone of the debate on corporate governance in the UK, in the accusations of executive greed in the US and deep distrust of business in France, Italy, Japan, the evidence is everywhere to be believed. Social legitimacy has been lost even though the notion of 'stakeholding' is trying to resurrect it. In the nuclear industry companies have to 'earn' their licence to operate.

Repsol, one of the healthiest and best-managed Spanish companies, earns about $900,000 in revenues and $32,000 in net income per employee. The corresponding figures for another oil company, Royal Dutch/Shell are $1.25 million and $160,000 respectively. To arrive at a similar enviable performance, Repsol will need to reduce employment by 40 per cent! Historically a cradle-to-grave employer, the company will have to derail its long-term commitments as an employer and as a key 'establishment' company in Spain.

Hence the response to the dilemma is the new moral contract that corporations must set about building with their employees. In Toyota and Samsung, IBM and Philips, the contract used to be job security traded off against loyalty and obedience – employees abiding by the rules of the organization and executing with diligence the tasks allocated to them. With knowledge rather than capital as the prime strategic resource, it is now the front-line employees closest to the day-to-day operators who must take responsibility for the company's competitive performance.

So in this emerging new contract, each employee takes responsibility for putting in a best-in-class performance, in exchange for which top management undertakes to ensure not the dependence of employment security but the freedom of each individual's 'employability'. This is done by providing continuous learning and skill updating opportunities and creating stimulating internal environments that motivate.

This contract recognizes that market performance flows not from the omnipotent wisdom of top management but from the initiative, creativity and skills of all employees. For employees it means getting out there and embracing the invigorating force of continuous learning and personal development, with networking an essential ingredient.

Under the new contract empowerment and employability go hand-in-hand. Networking is critical to this link, truly the new ties that bind.

9 Conclusion: Networth via Networks

'Live in fragments no longer. Only connect.'   E. M. Forster

While I was a guest at a recent dinner party in Washington DC, and while putting the finishing touches to this book, I was struck not only by the care with which the host and hostess (both successful careerists) organized the 'placements' (or seating plan), but the care that had been taken with the guest list itself. The interconnectedness between the guests was truly amazing in the context of networking. There was an element of 'serendipity' in that the hosts could not possibly have known of a positive professional coincidence for one of the guests meeting me, but most of it was sheer 'enlightenment', having thought through who would be most useful for who, complicated by husband and wife teams and unattached guests. Yet everyone was appropriate to the purpose of the dinner and it was fun and stylish. What's more it was put together with precision, and I was able to help someone who would later help an organization in which I am involved. I also met someone very important to one of the 'hats' I wear. Everyone gained, it was win-win for the guests and particularly the hosts, who had thought through not only the mutuality of interest, but the chemistry to the utmost.

During that particular trip I was wearing six different 'hats' – speaking at a conference, holding trade meetings, interviewing for staff, trying to persuade a university to partner a project, reviewing a possible joint venture and attending an important official dinner. The key in this kind of situation is to engineer your time and contacts, and creatively 'imagine' the links so they become a self-fulfilling prophecy. In addition I met some people on a social weekend with connections in the US, UK, India and South Africa who could potentially be helpful in a variety of ways – wheels within potential wheels.

Apart from running out of cards (law number 11!), pre-planning whom I should meet in each of these situations, what information I had to impart, what I sought and the follow-up (sorting the cards I was given), the critical path towards achieving the goals after the trip was vital to success. It is about everything from thank-you letters to whom to involve at the next step with what briefing, as well as to reflect on what you've learned, whom you've met and where the gaps are for next time.

I deliberately took a member of my trade association to a dinner in another field because I thought it would pay dividends for him; and it did, as well as being enjoyable. At one of my daytime meetings, I met the best friend of one of my colleagues at a company where I am Director, head-quartered in Washington, both of whom belong to the Junior League of Washington Women, a volunteer group – a network. Of course it is a small town! So coincidences are inevitable.

Ed Garlich, Managing Director of the Washington Research Group, an investment research and analysis company says, 'The name of the game in Washington is information and individuals. But while the information (thanks to IT) is out there, it's meeting the right people that counts.' In fact the key to a town like Washington, a one-horse political town, is think-tanks and lobby groups which feed on information, driven by networks. They act as a counterpoint to the formal, more hierarchical and bureau-cratic structures which are the more formal levers of the Federal government.

The Citizen Energy Alert network is a grassroots group of individuals concerned about America's energy future. It was set up, like all networks with a purpose, to provide people across the country with information and co-ordinate lobbying legislators. The network acts as a clearing house for information and as a catalyst for contact, a classic definition of a network that becomes institutionalized.

Georgia State Professor Thomas Stanley studied 2,000 millionaires and found the common denominator to be a huge Rolodex and an 'uncanny ability to distinguish quality contacts'. Collecting business cards is useless unless sorted for a resource pool of people, advice, ideas and support. Putting someone in touch with a third party may not immediately pay div-idends, but apart from the satisfaction of being the bridge-builder it will reap eventual rewards. A phrase which always leaves a little scratch on my mind is 'Never ask of others that which you yourself are unwilling to give!' Jump-starting to a smooth stop in networking does not involve ignoring those whose name tags don't fit your profile of a 'heavy hitter'. Working a room works both ways. 'Nothing loses a network more quickly than abus-ing it' is another truism.

One of the best networks a group of us initiated was my old school class reunion twenty-five years on. Nearly all of us had become successful (most as some sort of consultant, a sign of the times) and one even a rich company chairman (sceptical of so many consultants), another a headhunter (always useful). Of course networks with no purpose, other than an occasional reunion, lack the purpose or glue to hold such a network together! So we meet irregularly, though one or two bilateral relationships have thrived (one personal, the other a bit of both).

The value of networking is often appreciated late – when a career is in crisis. Therefore network before you need. It is at that point individuals

NETWORK BEFORE YOU NEED TO

may realize they have a poor understanding of their position in the market, having been too busy marketing their company, as that gruelling schedule – 'My diary (or calendar) is always full' – left them with few opportunities to meet others, inside or outside their organization.

Susan Bloch says, 'Just as organizations need to measure performance of key processes, individuals need to do the same if they are to manage their careers successfully.' Who am I and where am I now (self-awareness, not mirror-image is critical here), where do I want to get to, how do I get there, are key skills. In all this, networking is a crucial element.

As Reginald Watts, former co-author of *Corporate Revolution* says, 'The old boys' network was very restricted. Modern networking is far more organized, derived from a more meritocratic society like the US, treating the building of relationships as a management exercise in itself.' He is one of the best networkers I know, because even though by his own admission he is hopeless at remembering names, he makes notes, follows up by fixing breakfast, which he says conveys a different signal to lunch, let alone dinner. In fact his secretary always said that those people who couldn't get up in time for a breakfast meeting with him as a general rule wouldn't be the sort where there would be a mutual advantage anyway! Whenever you do it, it has to be managed as well as hopefully being interesting and fun.

Bernard Wynne calls networking 'a way of cutting through the crap'. His experience, which I endorse, is that the more you move around business the more you find people tap the same network, using those who are psychologically available. Nine out of ten are not accessible and protective of their position. How often people say 'That's not in my job spec!' In the US they are called 'Weebees' – we will be here when you come and still here when you go. Keep clear of them because there are other fish to fry.

It's understandable that people always stick to what and therefore who they know preferring to chat up someone with whom they have chemistry rather than take the plunge. What happens when you enter the room – you go up to the first person you know, when in fact you should act as host, even if you are a guest. Just as you feel better and are more successful if you do things ahead of time rather than at the last minute, similarly with networking beyond your circle of friends and easy-to-get-along-with colleagues, and before you need to call in the favour, you are more likely to be able to offer something if you have a wider net – information, gossip, other contacts, advice, anecdotes and even jokes.

This changes your whole mind-set. Think about it. If you are a consultant it's no good chatting to other consultants, except at a professional meeting, so if you need to, seek out those who are helpful in their networks, which is partly serendipity (like the friend who thoroughly enjoyed himself networking at two funerals in one week), but mainly enlightenment – pre-planning, research, a thoughtful approach, focus and action. It is more than just turning up to Studio 54 in New York for a 'Business Networking Seminar', putting your card in a doorside box and working the room!

If you and your organization want to achieve a goal, particularly at the grass roots level, a 'flexible and fungible' perspective is essential, because those you need to reach are outside your industry and your knowledge base. Whatever the purpose of the network personally, corporately or in alliance the truth is targeting – time, place and message and a smile helps. As Al Capone said (allegedly) 'You can get a better result with a smile and a gun than just a smile.'

Even in the tangled web (characterized as a system of alliances among corporations, limited partnerships, special joint ventures and project team-nets), the power becomes the power of colleagues or individuals rather than the power of positions or corporate structures.

So whatever your position as part of an organization or sole trader there is no substitute for effort and energy, being good at what you do and getting known for it. Lords Peter Gummer and Maurice Saatchi in the UK didn't get where they are today in the advertising and PR industries simply because they were beneficiaries of the 'halo effect' of advising the British Prime Minister, but became great at their jobs, including networking. Networking is not some quick fix nor can it be seen in isolation.

Sir David Frost, the Concorde junkie ('Concorde is the best network in the world') now picks up the phone to interview anyone, as does Barbara Walters, or better still people beat a path to *their* door. They can do this not just because they are good networkers, but because they are talented and have always been good networkers as an integral part of that talent.

Not everyone is David Frost or Barbara Walters. But you can jump-start your network by identifying ten key contacts essential to you over the next year, check the list out with colleagues, focus on those contacts, review progress and by the end of the year the network should have grown to 100. This is ideal for a start-up situation and to achieve short-term goals. But ultimately a strategic approach is required, lest the network becomes too narrowly focused; and of course there are different ways of keeping in touch. Ultimately, make the most of the support of mentors, colleagues, friends and family. Excel at monitoring colleagues so they become co-conspirators. It's less stressful and more exhilarating to own your own career, to truly be an autonomous employee.

Apart from taking control of a career, more and more people are becoming 'single-minded' in terms of their private lives. In the UK one in three households will be a single adult by the end of the century, requiring a new approach to networking. A number of new organizations have emerged for people who simply want to make friends with other singles of either sex. The purpose of the network is to have fun, only secondarily to find a partner. Similar organizations have existed in large alienating cities like New York for years, a convergence of two social trends, affluence and overcrowding.

Even though most people in China and Vietnam are young, in the US the population is ageing, with the number of over-65s more than tripled since 1900. Yet most marketeers still treat them as only buying a Buick and a casket as major purchases between now and their deaths. Not so; and with healthier, wealthier and more mobile lives they are needing to update their Rolodexes too!

In the US in particular, with more leisure time and the inability of the government to solve all problems, there's a growing volume of community service volunteers – mainly women who share information, listen and make an impact in the community. 'Connect America' is a new group set up to build bridges between different 'stakeholders' in local communities.

Just as it requires a willingness to be 'involved' by each member of a personal network, based on mutual respect and maintaining confidences, so too in corporate alliances each company should know that hurting the other damages the alliance and that trust is essential, because alliances are between people.

The British Nuclear Industry Forum has led several delegations to China in recent years. Apart from being late in the day compared to some other national competitors, the British are highly regarded. But whoever you are it's vital for the industry to understand not just the structure of the appropriate networks but the long-term cultural approaches as well as who fits where – a question of pooling intelligence: information, interface, issues = influence.

Trade associations provide neutral territory for competitors to share information, but it could also lead to resource sharing. Consultants are also a useful source to tap as by definition their network is large, especially as they tend to occupy a pivotal role in rapidly changing business environments.

Building an informal link with customers can also be useful for feedback. Finding an external mentor is another option at whatever stage in the career progression. Building relationships with superstars is helpful because they are already at the front of the crowd. It is also important to network with those who have a different social reference point so as not to cut yourself off from the mainstream into some privileged enclave; this takes courage but is worth the investment. Indeed if you want to expand your sphere of influence, it's absolutely essential.

Networking must be of mutual benefit. Quality and integrity are vital ingredients. Listening is critical not just for information but ideas, inspiration and insights as well as learning the other point of view. It's about trust, not trade; relationships, not transactions; giving, not taking; long-term, not short-term. It should not stand in the way of delivering performance, but should be integral to daily personal and corporate lives in a balanced and productive way. Networking doesn't guarantee success in these turbulent times with greater complexity and difficulties of definition. But a confident information, interfaces and issues management in a focused and targeted way leads to influence. Hence the value of networking. But it's not just about work; it will bring balance to your personal and corporate life, because it's predicated on focusing your energy. Giving without expectation is not a game to be played, but if undertaken in the right spirit networks which get together get ahead, in a personal as well as a professional sense.

The founder of the World Economic Forum, Klaus Schwab, summing up the last Davos Symposium, said if he were granted three wishes it would be that each delegate made at least one important business contact, went home with one important idea and found one real new friend, which to me summarizes what networking is all about. It's not 'unidimensional'. The key to networking is what you put into it – win/win, reciprocity and mutuality.

Just as the best-managed companies network internally with the best work done via informal channels, so too external networking differentiates you from the crowd and teaches you about yourself. It's not possible to take an undisciplined or dilettante approach. To be successful on a sustainable basis requires a holistic approach, an ability to see the big picture – building a lifelong support system. Use time and energy to keep and learn from people.

Women are finding it an invaluable tool and are indeed moving its frontiers. The coming together post-Cold War of Asian values with Western capitalist democracy in a global market economy will impact how we function together and help us make the connections in economic, social and political terms, increasingly on a global and not just a local or national basis. I have referred to 'netmapping'. We all operate and communicate from our own personal maps of reality. What we have to do as individuals or corporations is change those maps to get it right; a map that provides the widest options and richest support and helping others do the same networking therefore is a state of mind, a way of behaving, a philosophy even. I'll let you know in my next book how well my *current* networking served me: personally, professionally, in my companies and in the organization where I work. People always say to me after a reversal of fortune how quickly I pick myself up. Networking is a key part of the equation, access to decision-takers, timely information, and above all, support.

I believe even more, having written this book, that networking is susceptible to a systematic approach. I have tried to cut the cake from a variety of perspectives, cultural, corporate, personal and professional. Some networking notables have said to me that it goes against the spirit of networking to make it analytical and clinical, prescribing it in an unfortunate way. I trust I have proved my hypothesis however without taking it too seriously, while raising it above the level of merely, 'How to work the room'. Via anecdote and some methodology I have looked at the management aspects, self-help and its morality, hopefully without becoming obsessive.

Maybe after all it is a question of enlightened serendipity. But above all if purpose is the glue, trust is the grease of networking.

Bibliography

Clutterbuck, D. & Goldsmith, W. (1984). *The Winning Streak*. Weidenfeld & Nicolson.

Clutterbuck, D. & Dearlove, D. (1991). *Routes to the Top*. Kinsley Lord.

Covey, Dr S. (1989). *The Seven Habits of Highly Effective People*. Simon & Schuster.

DEMOS/MORI. 'Freedom's Children: Work Relations and Politics Report'.

Drucker, P. (1993). *Post Capitalist Society*. Butterworth Heinemann.

Forster, E. M. *Howard's End*.

Fukuyama, F. (1995). *Trust: the Social Virtues and the Creation of Prosperity*. Hamish Hamilton, Penguin Books.

Handy, C. (1989). *The Age of Unreason*. Harvard Business School Press.

Hayes, R. & Watts, R. (1984). *Corporate Revolution*. Heinemann.

Levitt, T. (1986). *The Marketing Imagination*. The Free Press.

Limerick, D. & Cunnington, A. (1993). *Managing the New Organisation: A Blueprint for Networks and Strategic Alliances*. Business & Professional Publishing.

Lipnack, J. & Stamps, J. (1994). *The Age of the Network: Organising Principles for the 21st Century*. Oliver Wight.

McKenna, R. (1985). *The Regis Touch*. Addison Wesley.

Moss Kanter, R. (July/August 1994). 'Collaborative Advantage', *Harvard Business Review*.

Naisbitt, J. (1996). *Megatrends Asia: Eight Asian Megatrends that are Reshaping Our World*. Simon & Schuster.

Ohmae, K. (1995). *The End of the Nation State: The Rise of Regional Economies*. The Free Press/McKinsey & Co.

Ohmae, K. (March/April 1989). 'The Global Logic of Strategic Alliances', *Harvard Business Review*.

Peters, T. (1992). *Liberation Management: Necessary Disorganisation for the Nanosecond Nineties*. Pan Books.

Putnam, R. (1996). 'Bowling Alone: America's Declining Social Capital' essay. American Political Science Association.

Reich, R. (1991). *The Work of Nations: Preparing Ourselves for 21st Century Capitalism*. Simon & Schuster.

Royal Society of Arts Inquiry (1995). 'Tomorrow's Company: The Role of Business in a Changing World'.

Sumantra, G. & Bartlett, Prof. C. 'The World in 1996', *The Economist* publication. London & Harvard Business School.

Toffler, A. (1990). *Knowledge, Wealth and Violence at the Edge of the 21st Century*. Bantam Books.

Index